W9-CHU-814

Not for Free

NOT FOR
FREE

*Revenue Strategies
for a New World*

Saul J. Berman

Harvard Business Review Press

Boston, Massachusetts

Library of Congress Cataloging-in-Publication Data

Berman, Saul Jay, 1946-
  Not for free : making money in the digital age / by Saul J. Berman.
    p. cm.
  ISBN 978-1-4221-3167-1 (hbk. : alk. paper)
1. Market segmentation. 2. New products. 3. Technological innovations. 4. Digital media—Economic aspects. I. Title.
  HF5415.127.B45 2011
  658.8'02—dc22

                               2010031417

CONTENTS

Introduction   **1**
Nothing's Free: Revenue Challenges,
Revenue Opportunity

1 **Segmentation**   **21**

2 **Pricing Innovation**   **65**

3 **Payer Innovation**   **109**

4 **Package Innovation**   **143**

Conclusion   **171**
Launching Innovation

Notes   *193*
Index   *203*
Acknowledgments   *217*
About the Author   *223*

Nothing's Free

Revenue Challenges, Revenue Opportunity

Back in the days of the dot-com bust, it was common to mock entrepreneurs and investors for thinking they could be successful without a clear and credible plan for how their business would make money. Those taunts of start-ups and spin-offs were deserved. Yet over the last decade we've seen established companies with decades of success suddenly find themselves in the same position—without a business model that fits the reality of their competitive market.

Business model disruption is rampant, not because companies have stopped offering products that people want but because consumers stopped being willing to pay for many products at the same levels in the same ways. "Free" took hold of consumer consciousness in no small part because of the hollow promises given by many Internet start-ups. Those first affected by the phenomenon of free, including many businesses in the media industry, have experienced dramatic consequences: the music record labels saw revenue declines of 40 percent from their 2000 high; newspapers lost 85 percent of classified revenue from their print editions between 2005 and 2009; and long-distance telecommunications revenues declined by 80 percent in the first decade of the century.[1] Venerable companies like Warner Music and Time Inc. have started to look a lot more like Pets.com than anyone could have imagined ten years ago. Even nonmedia industries are more affected by free than most would like to admit, as industries as far flung as retail banking, software, and consumer electronics have been pressured to sweeten their offerings with "free" add-ons, additional functionality, and lower prices.

Many traditional companies have spent the past decade doing their best imitation of the little Dutch boy using his finger to plug the hole in the dike. Cable providers such as Time Warner Cable and Cablevision are fighting with content providers over the fees they pay for programming, resulting in a number of high-profile channel blackouts, including one in New York on Oscar night. *Time* magazine is implementing a new paywall model as I write this that will require readers to have some type of subscription to read a story, either to the physical magazine or through an iPad. And the *New York Times* felt that shifting away from free was so difficult, it needed to announce a change in pricing almost a year in advance. The net outcome of these examples seems to be baffled and belligerent customers, confused partners, and less than stellar revenue results.

Yet these examples only offer part of the story. A number of stories coming out of the media industry and elsewhere also show companies going beyond free, and succeeding. These efforts largely involve innovations around the revenue model—the pricing of products, how they are packaged, and who pays for them. Those are the stories I'll tell in this book.

Learning from Media

I suspect that many executives struggling with stagnant or falling revenue, tight credit, and uncertain prospects for growth have taken some solace in the fact that they are not in the media industry. The struggles experienced by many sectors of media are well known: shrinking revenues, consumers who steal the product and then distribute it freely, rapid technology change, competition from a range of sources, and supply chain disruptions and defections. Almost everything that could go wrong for music, magazine publishing, radio, newspapers, and broadcast television has gone wrong in the last fifteen years.

Of course, some of the damage to these sectors has been self-inflicted. From music suing its biggest fans over piracy and then refusing to take the opportunity to sell individual songs as well as albums, to print newspapers waffling between giving content away for free and charging for it, it seems that media has not missed an opportunity to miss an opportunity. Infrequently has any sector in the industry learned from the experience of another sector. As one television executive I spoke to recently told me, "Music may have gotten hit by a bus when peer-to-peer sharing blew up the revenue model, but television is just committing suicide."

It's easy from the outside to engage in a bit of schadenfreude and simply dismiss media's experience as the result of unique circumstances and poor management. That would be a mistake. The reality is that the external and internal factors affecting media are not unique to the sector. In fact, media is the proverbial canary in the coal mine for all sorts of industries. The external trends driving change to the sector are:

- Ubiquitous low-cost communications

- Virtually unlimited low-cost bandwidth

- Virtually unlimited, low-cost, real-time data processing power

- Consumer expectations for personalization, control, relevance, and timeliness

- Rapid technological and competitive innovation

These trends affect many businesses in most every industry. The magnitude and speed of those effects vary, of course, but no industry is immune.

In terms of internal causes, executives in the media industry are neither uniquely shortsighted nor complacent and greedy. The organizational, even human, dynamics that led to many of the mistakes and poor decisions are shared. Numerous influential books and articles drawing from all industries have documented how and why people fail to see challenges and opportunities, execute necessary change, and innovate new solutions: *Good to Great, Blue Ocean Strategy, The Innovator's Dilemma, The Origin and Evolution of New Businesses, When Growth Stalls, Switch,* and *Leading Change.*

Furthermore, the story of the modern media industry isn't just a litany of failure. Music, print media, radio, and broadcast

FIGURE I-1

U.S. media projected growth, 2008–2012

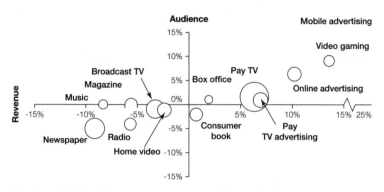

Note: Size of bubble = 2008 revenues: revenue streams include advertising.

Sources: Veronis Suhler Stevenson Communications Forecast 2009; IBM Institute for Business Value analysis.

television have taken a beating in recent years, especially during the recession. Some companies have their worst years still ahead of them. But others have prospered (see figure I-1). Video gaming has seen double-digit growth. Mobile advertising is expected to explode. Google, Amazon, and Apple are well-known success stories, with growing portions of their revenue streams and value propositions derived from media. Beyond those well-chronicled companies, there are also examples like Redbox (which has captured an 18 percent share of the video rental market in just a few years) and the *Financial Times*, which has grown revenue while its sector peers have seen their incomes crash.[2] Then there are Pandora, Blyk, Spotify, Hulu, Gawker Media, and many other undeniable success stories.

There are lessons to be learned from the media industry, both positive and negative, about how to cope with the economic environment and business context trends that all industries are facing. Those lessons are the focus of this book.

More specifically, I focus on the business model innovations that are required for any company to be successful in an environment of ubiquitous communications, virtually unlimited bandwidth and processing power, changed consumer expectations, and rapid innovation. Business model innovation is a broad topic, so I'm going to focus specifically on the revenue side of the business model equation.

There are countless definitions of *business model*, and I have no ambition to provide a definitive one.[3] What almost all the definitions share is a view that a business model encompasses how a firm creates value, how it delivers that value to customers, and how it captures revenue from those customers. Value creation, value delivery, and revenue capture are obviously interlinked. Changing the revenue model may require changes to how the firm creates and delivers value, and vice versa. Still, it's useful to define business models as including these three broad functions.

Business model innovation likewise takes multiple forms (see figure I-2). The annual CEO study that I run with my colleagues at IBM defines three main business model innovation approaches: industry innovation, enterprise innovation, and revenue innovation. There isn't a one-to-one match between the three functions of a business model and the three types of business model innovation, unfortunately. Just as the functions overlap, these types of business model innovation often involve two or more of the functions.

Industry innovation happens when a firm crosses the boundary from one industry to another. For instance, Virgin's move

FIGURE I-2

IBM framework for business model innovation

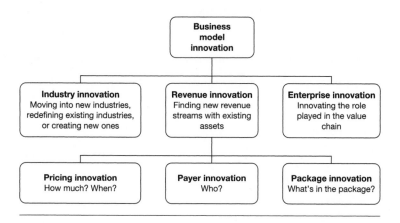

from music retail into transportation and financial services, along with the focus on high-quality customer service it brought to those industries, was an industry innovation. Likewise, a company is engaging in industry innovation when it creates an entirely new industry, as Google has done with the search market and as Microsoft did by catalyzing the personal computer industry.

Enterprise innovation in turn involves rethinking the way the firm defines its boundaries. Zara and Li & Fung offer good examples within the apparel industry. In the case of Zara, it expanded the boundaries of the typical apparel firm with its decision to own every aspect of the apparel value chain, so that it could respond quickly to emerging fashion trends. In contrast, Li & Fung dramatically shrank the boundaries of an apparel manufacturing firm by functioning as a service provider that links buyers with a vast network of independent apparel manufacturers. As a result, it offers clients a level of flexibility that it never could have if it owned factories.

Revenue innovation focuses on how the firm captures revenues from the value it creates with its existing assets. Revenue innovation involves three distinct issues: how the value is priced, how the value is packaged, and who is paying for the value. While there have always been myriad approaches to these issues, the general trends of communications and computing ubiquity, along with the change in consumer expectations that has come about partly as a result of the former two trends and the availability of information, have rapidly expanded the possible approaches and therefore the opportunity for innovation.

There are a number of reasons to focus on revenue innovation. The first is its relative simplicity. Industry innovation, enterprise innovation, and revenue innovation are all complex and difficult to achieve, but each is less complex than the one before. For industries and firms that are struggling with stagnant or declining revenue, there is an urgent need to stem, if not stop, the bleeding. Revenue innovation offers the fastest business model innovation path to new revenue streams, certainly far faster and less expensive than the effort required for industry and enterprise innovation.

Second, in situations where industries are being radically transformed or firms are facing bankruptcy or collapse and more extensive business model innovation is required, revenue innovation can often provide several vital benefits: (a) generate funding for more extensive innovation efforts by locating new sources of revenue from existing assets; (b) provide needed insight into how customers and markets are changing, which will guide further innovation; and (c) give a reeling company a few short-term wins and, with them, the confidence it needs to drive more extensive change. Revenue innovation can be a powerful antidote to the fourth stage of decline documented by Jim Collins in *How the Mighty Fall*, where companies often cast wildly about trying to find "salvation."[4]

The third reason to pursue revenue innovation is that it allows for smaller-scale, shorter-term experiments. These efforts help firms identify key talent and unexpected barriers to innovation, and they allow them to derive lessons to apply to more intensive innovation efforts.

In short, revenue innovation matters. Likewise, the media industry is worth looking to for revenue innovation lessons and successes. Nonmedia companies may question the connection, but media has more in common with nonmedia industries than the latters' executives may care to admit. The commonality lies in the major trends that have dramatically changed the environment for media companies. As noted, those trends are ubiquitous communications; virtually unlimited low-cost bandwidth; virtually unlimited low-cost data processing power; changing consumer expectations for personalization, control, relevance, and timeliness; and rapid technological and competitive innovation.

These are all recursive trends—each builds on and extends the others. Processing power in part underlies the rise of ubiquitous communications and low-cost bandwidth. The data and information produced by ubiquitous communications and low-cost bandwidth likewise drive demand for data processing power, further accelerating that trend. Put together, these trends had a major impact on the media industry. The primary product of media could be digitized. So long as processing power and bandwidth were limited and expensive, the product stayed analog, along with all the attendant limitations of physical manufacture and delivery. Once thresholds of processing power and bandwidth were crossed, however, the product broke free from its physical bounds. Not only that, it could be acquired in near real time. The shift to digital and the real-time nature of modern transactions changed the dynamics of the industry. Music was the first to feel the effects, but the tremors quickly reverberated to all parts of the industry.

These trends do not affect only industries whose product can be wholly digitized. For all industries, the rise of ubiquitous communications, virtually unlimited low-cost bandwidth, virtually unlimited low-cost processing power, and changing consumer expectations means that vastly more information is flowing to and from customers, so that even physical products can now have a useful information component. Take, for instance, the automotive industry's pursuit of information services like GM's OnStar and Ford's Sync. Those are digitized information products attached to a quintessential physical product. Or consider the wide range of industrial tool companies that now offer remote monitoring and preventive maintenance services to extend the life of their physical products.

Look as well to health care. A great deal of the argument made in 2010 by those in favor of U.S. health-care reform focused on the cost savings and care improvements that would come by collecting and applying better information: electronic health records can prevent duplicate tests and fraudulent claims; comparative effectiveness data will allow doctors to prescribe less expensive treatments that work just as well; and information from the developing genome sector may in the future help identify in advance the 43 percent of diabetes patients for whom current drugs are ineffective.[5]

This increased information flow is set to grow even more rapidly in the decade ahead as the "Internet of things" that futurists have discussed for the last decade begins to find application in the real world. Over time, more devices will be connected to information networks able to create or react to data. The firm I work for, IBM, bundles these trends together under the rubric of a "Smarter Planet"—a phrase that suggests a world where information is created and consumed everywhere.

The ubiquity of information hinted at by a Smarter Planet drives another of the major trends: increasing consumer demand for personalization, control, relevance, and timeliness. While there's no doubt that these demands have always been latent in consumers, the ubiquity of low-cost communications, bandwidth, and processing power have allowed those latent desires to rise to the fore because those desires can now be met. When communications and bandwidth were expensive, information flowed primarily one way: from producer to consumer. Today, producers can cheaply gather information about not only how many units of a product are sold but how, when, and by whom those products are bought and how, when, and by whom those products are used. Combining that information with cheap data processing power yields the ability to profitably customize products to ever-smaller groups of consumers. As those latent desires are met, consumers will expect that even more of the products they use fulfill their expectations of personalization, control, relevance, and timeliness. Producers that do not deliver to those expectations will lose to those that do.

It hardly bears mentioning that every industry is confronting rapid technological and competitive innovation.

The sum of these trends makes business model innovation critical for growth and success. There is strong research to support this conclusion based on some analysis my colleagues and I at the IBM Institute for Business Value performed when following up on one of our annual CEO surveys. The CEO respondents said unsurprisingly that they expected the competitive and business environment to get more challenging. Many of them also said they were confronting those challenges by focusing on "innovation." But innovation can mean many things—in most cases, when companies mention innovation, they are talking about innovating products; they are not innovating around business models.

So we decided to clarify what types of innovation CEOs were focused on and whether that focus was having a material effect on performance. We found that the firms with the fastest profit growth compared to competitors' over the previous three years had put twice as much emphasis on business model innovation as the average firm in the sample. That's a powerful argument for moving business model innovation higher on your agenda.[6]

Let me also offer a few reasons why I think the experience of media is important to understand and learn from for those seeking insight into business model innovations generally and revenue model innovations in particular. The biggest reason is hinted at in figure I-1, shown earlier. In the figure you'll note that a number of sectors in the industry are in the upper-right quadrant, meaning they are expected to grow their audiences and revenues. In the midst of the "perfect storm" some sectors are profiting. You'll also note that substantial portions of the industry are competing for the preeminent position on the lower left—indicating falling audience and shrinking revenues.

This same chart could be duplicated for individual companies, and the same spread would appear. Some companies are growing audience and revenues—even in challenged sectors—while their peers seem trapped in a downward spiral.

The distribution of success and failure in the media industry is not random. There are ways that portions of the industry have ridden the challenging environment, fought off the negative side of the trends, and succeeded. Likewise, there are strategies and reactions that have failed miserably. Given that the major trends of ubiquitous communications, unlimited low-cost bandwidth, and so on are affecting all industries, learning what worked and what didn't in the media industry will be useful in the development of planning strategies for your company. It's like getting an advance map of previously uncharted territory: you can see where the roadblocks are, why some "surefire" innovations never caught fire, and why some "that'll never work" strategies caught hold.

Another major reason to look to media is that its lessons are already being applied to many other industries. As you move through the book, you'll find that I've documented cases of revenue innovations attempted by media that have been introduced to good effect in other industries. These case studies illustrate the commonalities and differences in revenue innovation as it is applied across various industries. Table I-1 has a sampling of the industries and companies that are using revenue innovation today to improve their top and bottom lines.

TABLE I-1

Revenue innovations outside the media industry

Innovation	Nonmedia industry firm
Segmentation	• Automotive: Better Place, Zipcar
	• Consumer utilities: Ontario Hydro
	• Retail grocery: Tesco, Costco
	• Casinos: Harrahs
Pricing innovation	• Apparel: Rent the Runway
	• Retail: Amazon Prime
	• Pharmaceutical: Johnson & Johnson, Merck
	• Automotive insurance: Progressive
	• Automotive rental: Zipcar
	• Financial services: Mint.com
Payer innovation	• Mobile telecommunications: Blyk, O2
	• Retail: Walmart
	• Consumer packaged goods: Procter & Gamble
Package innovation	• Logistics: Vessel Tracker
	• Food: Nespresso
	• Apparel/shoes: Nike, Converse
	• Consumer electronics: Apple, Amazon, Google
	• Flooring: Interface

Fortunately, a wide variety of innovations have been attempted in the media industry, which is another reason why it can offer useful lessons. Companies have tried a huge range of innovations and strategies, similar to the heterogeneity of outcomes experienced in the industry. To paraphrase Walt Disney, "If you can dream it, they did it": free, not free, freemium, customized, one size fits all, low cost, high cost, componentized, bundled, sponsored, ad supported, and on and on.

Finally, companies in all industries have an opportunity to get ahead of the curve. Some of the experiences and lessons of the media industry may not apply to your company or industry, but most do. At the very least, they can challenge you to rethink your assumptions about what works or does not work. The key to successful innovation is breaking through our fundamental assumptions to see things in an entirely new way. As Tim Brown, CEO of IDEO, one of the most respected innovation consulting firms in the world, has said, "We human beings are not particularly good at solving our own problems."[7] To really solve problems, it often helps to get an outside perspective—in this case, to view your industry through the lens of another.

If your industry has not yet been deeply affected by, for instance, a shift in value from atoms to bits, from physical products to information, then view this book as a set of ideas for how you can introduce those innovations successfully and generate new revenue streams for your company. George Day, professor of marketing at the Wharton School and chairman of the American Marketing Association, wrote in his book *Peripheral Vision* of the difficulty that many companies have detecting those "weak signals" from the market that are the harbingers of major change.[8] If you're in an industry that isn't in the throes of major change because of the trends I've discussed, consider this book part of your peripheral vision. It can give you a leg up on competitors who aren't picking up the (for now) weak signals of major change.

The Structure of the Book

Just as there are several types of business model innovation, there are several types of revenue model innovation. In the book, I've broken them down into three major categories and

FIGURE I-3

Revenue model innovation

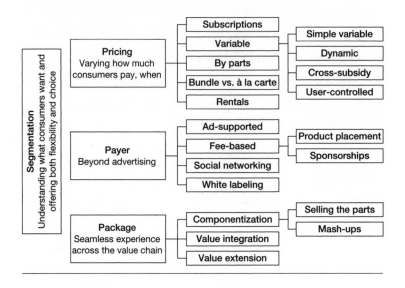

roughly organized the book around them. The three categories are pricing innovation, payer innovation, and package innovation (see figure I-3).

Pricing innovation looks at new ways to charge for your product—in terms of both the amount of money charged and the point (or points) in time when the customer is required to pay. Innovations around pricing use existing pricing models in nontraditional ways, such as à la carte pricing applied to the traditionally bundled cable industry, or they may add new twists on well-known pricing approaches.

Payer innovation looks at finding customers who are not ultimately the consumers of the product or altering *who* pays for a given good or service. The most common payer innovation is the use of indirect payment approaches, such as advertising and sponsorship. Given that, I'll dwell a bit on the future of the advertising industry and where ad-driven approaches are working and not working.

Package innovation looks at new ways to expand product or brand value to different customer behaviors and segments or different ways of offering the product to the customer. Examples of new packaging options that have come about as a consequence of digitization include componentization and mash-ups. But package innovation also opens opportunities for companies to add value at different points along the value chain, or to extend their value proposition to adjacent markets.

Before I drill into the varieties of revenue model innovation, however, we have to look at the foundation of all business models: customers. More specifically, we have to examine how to segment customers so that revenue model innovations can be appropriately targeted to those who will perceive value from the product and are willing and able to pay for it. The major trends of ubiquitous and cheap communications, bandwidth, information, and processing power have changed customer expectations, but they have also changed the ability to gather information about customers. A new and better segmentation based on that information is where revenue innovation has to start. I cover that topic in the first chapter of the book.

Each chapter is organized similarly. First there's a section that defines, describes, and offers examples of the different approaches to segmentation, pricing innovation, payer innovation, and package innovation, respectively. That descriptive section is followed by a "pitfalls" section, which communicates some of the challenges companies face when implementing the proposed models, and a "lessons" section, which offers suggestions of what companies can do to improve their chances at success. Each chapter closes with a series of questions aimed at stimulating thought and brainstorming to allow you to get started with your own revenue innovation experiments.

Some examples in each chapter are focused on media industry cases. These cases may at times seem overly detailed, but understanding why a company made certain choices or why innovations did or didn't work requires understanding those details. In all cases, the examples were chosen to offer ideas for those who are just starting to experiment with revenue innovation, and to create food for thought for executives in other industries.

My choice to organize the chapters around segmentation, pricing, payer, and package innovation was a function of convenience and simplicity. In real life, however, revenue innovation can't be so simply implemented in neat little boxes. In practice, pricing, payer, and package innovations are not mutually exclusive. They are parts of a moving system, one or all of which can be put in motion at any given time. Advertising models will continue to cross-subsidize subscriptions, for example, and both will be applied to new package innovations such as components.

In the conclusion, I offer examples for how the various revenue innovation models coexist and interact with each other, and take a look at the particular dynamics within industries and companies that may make one innovation model more appropriate than another for a particular context. I also include some tips on governance approaches companies can take to encourage or incubate innovation.

Introduction

I wrote this book to be a thought and discussion guide for executives and organizations looking to jump-start their experimentation with revenue innovation. The book frames the current context to allow readers to understand the types of revenue innovations, identify the key lessons that have come out of existing experiments (successful and failed) in revenue innovation, and ask the questions they need to start experimenting with their own products.

Most of the research for this book was conducted in conjunction with my colleagues at IBM, and I draw heavily on IBM research. Many of the case studies from the media industry are from companies that I have come into contact with or actively watched in the media industry. By no means is this book a comprehensive history of the media industry or a complete look at business model innovation. The best innovation comes from doing, not reading. I hope this book gives you just enough, and never too much, to start innovating your revenue models in an informed and successful way.

1

Segmentation

I n 2003, the home movie rental industry suddenly shifted. Blockbuster Video had led the market for more than fifteen years with a network of retail outlets whose in-store inventory tended toward newer, popular releases, rented at $4.99 for three days or so. This physical, time-limited model made visiting Blockbuster a lot like going to the public library: the clientele was diverse; the odds of getting a movie you wanted were fifty-fifty; and late fees were steep. Still, the pay-per-rental revenue model for video rental was the only option.

Then, in 2003, Netflix launched a subscription-based Internet movie rental service that uprooted Blockbuster's dominant position. Netflix had no physical stores, seemingly limitless inventory, an Internet management system that allowed customers to choose what movies they wanted in advance, and a convenient mail-based method for return and delivery that removed the need to drive to the store. Netflix also replaced the traditional pay-per-rental revenue model with a subscription structure. Customers signed up to receive between one and eight DVDs at a time, and they could opt to keep any DVD for as long as they wanted—no late fees. By 2009, Netflix had captured 36 percent of the rental market, and Blockbuster had added a mail-based subscription service of its own.[1]

Blockbuster's carefully constructed business model, based on retail ubiquity and new-release availability, was no longer of much use. In fact, its physical stores became a burden. Netflix made location much less relevant and, in so doing, exposed Blockbuster's limitations in inventory and time-flexibility. In short, Netflix upended Blockbuster's geographical segmentation.[2]

Segmentation and Revenue Innovation

Netflix's increased inventory and improved efficiency would not have yielded such a fundamental shift in the video rental industry if there hadn't been a segment of digital-savvy consumers who were ready to move away from the in-store experience toward Internet search and postal-mail management. New revenue models need customers who are ready to abandon their old ways of doing things. In the past, new entrants have almost always been the disrupters of existing industries. This concept has been widely written about by Clayton Christensen and others, and its primary cause lies in the fact that new entrants do not have existing revenues to protect, so they are not limited in how they pursue the customer. Yet the opportunity inherent to new entrants also exists for incumbents; it's just hard for them to see because they are locked into a particular (but often no longer relevant) view of the market, its segments, and their needs.

Segmentation for most companies means dividing customers into groups based on where they live or how old they are or their sex or their "lifestyle," but these approaches are not all that suggestive for digital consumers. These traditional segmentation approaches are at best correlative—they take an identifiable characteristic and match it with a likely behavior. Why be so indirect? Why not look directly for the behaviors relevant to your industry? Doing so can reveal when consumers are well served with an existing business model and when consumers would be open to new ways of doing things, especially for incumbents. Blockbuster didn't need to lose market share to Netflix to see an alternative segmentation and an alternative revenue model. It just needed to see some suggestive behaviors of a subset of customers. I don't have specific insight into Blockbuster's data, but one relevant sign might have come from customers who consistently returned rentals after their due dates. These customers likely lived at an inconvenient distance from a Blockbuster outlet, or their schedules didn't allow timely returns, or they were just forgetful. Blockbuster earned a lot of late fees at the expense of those customers, but it did not breed good will or loyalty. Mining data on those customers to see whether there were any measurable declines in rental activity after fines were assessed might have helped Blockbuster develop a differentiated view of its user base and innovate an alternative revenue model that could coexist with the retail model to serve that segment of customers.

Segmentation is a prerequisite for revenue innovation. None of what comes in the following chapters around alternative pricing, payer, and package models will work without first understanding the distinct categories into which your customers fall. But not just any segmentation will do. The following pages offer a brief history of traditional approaches to segmentation along with my case for a new approach built on actual behavior, including behavior around technology and information, rather than just correlations to easily observable characteristics. I outline a segmentation model I helped develop at IBM's Institute for Business Value as an example of how a behavioral segmentation like this might look within and outside of media. I then apply a behavioral segmentation view to the music industry and a number of sample nonmedia industries to demonstrate how a behavioral approach to segmentation could shift strategic business decisions and open the door for new revenue models.

Segmentation: A Brief History

Segmentation has existed in some form since the dawn of marketing. The post-WWII expansion of industry in the United States brought with it an increase in consumer options. In the words of Wendell Smith, the intellectual godfather of segmentation, consumers developed "different wants." Rather than view one market as a heterogeneous pool, Smith's early work on segmentation allowed marketers to view it as multiple, homogeneous markets.

Those homogeneous markets were pretty broad—"New Yorkers," for example, or "upper middle class." Geographic location or socioeconomic class was the primary basis along which marketers divided consumer groups. A *basis*, as defined by scholars Ronald Frank, William Massey, and Yoram Wind in the 1970s, is a characteristic that can be used to place customers into distinct homogeneous pools.[3] For decades, demographic, geographic, and socioeconomic bases drove market segmentation practices. Psychographic segmentation became popular in the 1980s after futurist Arnold Mitchell of the Stanford Research Institute (SRI International) launched the Values and Lifestyle (VALS) methodology, based on Abraham Maslow's hierarchy of needs. VALS were not a replacement for more tangible demographic segmentation bases—observable characteristics like geography and sex were simply too easy to identify, and they stayed stable over long periods of time. But ultimately, both demographic and VALS segmentations are based on relatively weak correlations between characteristics and behaviors.

The purpose of segmentation is to help companies understand what their customers want so they can develop targeted strategies and specific products that are more likely to succeed. Yet few companies really do that. There are the famous exceptions, such as Johnson & Johnson and Procter & Gamble. But for most companies, segmentation has served more often to develop a tactical marketing plan for existing products or to justify decisions after the fact. Most damningly, years of scholarship have failed to identify a reliable, predictive link between broad demographic categories and purchasing behavior.[4]

Nonetheless, companies still use them, for lack of a more reliable and cost-effective alternative. In media, the use of demographic bases has allowed broadcast stations since the 1950s to adjust programming by time of day to suit the dominant audience: daytime talk shows and soap operas for stay-at-home women, "family programs" for the evening, adult police or hospital dramas for late prime time. The dominant segmentation in media has been determined almost entirely by two bases: age and sex.

Age and sex have largely operated as a proxy for taste. Men between the ages of eighteen and thirty-four like sports, for example, or women between the ages of thirty-five and forty-five like romantic films. Neither of those statements is always true, of course, but they are true often enough that companies could develop marketing plans and revenue models around them.

Exceptions have been ignored. Until recently, there was no easy way to identify customers who fell outside the age-and-sex or VALS norms, and the packaging limitations of most analog products made it too expensive to deliver customized products to finer segments anyway. Besides, the age-and-sex approach seemed as good as any. In a world where consumers only had the choice to either watch or not watch, they watched: in the 1970s, a well-placed prime-time television commercial could expect to reach at least 80 percent of the viewing public in any given region.[5]

A lot has changed in the past thirty years. For one thing, consumers are no longer watching (or listening to, or reading) the same thing as their neighbors or their basis cohorts. The 1980s saw an initial dip to 70 percent audience penetration for a well-placed television ad, and the numbers plummeted from there.

Today, ideal TV ad placement will capture only 35 percent of consumers.

Part of this audience erosion has come from a proliferation of content and channels. With the exception of the one-night-a-year Super Bowl and other live events like the Olympics, no program today captures the majority of viewers the way *M*A*S*H* or *Dallas* did in their prime. There are too many options catering to distinct tastes, with *Iron Chef* going head-to-head with *Project Runway*, *Masterpiece Mystery!*, *Law & Order Special Victims Unit*, and syndicated reruns of *The Fresh Prince of Bel-Air*.

Working on a Behavioral Basis

Audience fragmentation is a real phenomenon. Yet a more significant factor affecting consumer consumption patterns is the change in consumer expectations. Consumers have come to expect ever-increasing convenience, flexibility, relevance, and customization. This is a consequence of, among other factors, rapid technology advances (as detailed in the introduction) that have enabled companies to incrementally begin meeting those expectations.

With digitization, content has become independent from specific physical delivery formats. News has been freed from the paper, music from the CD, sitcoms from the television set. Viewers are no longer deciding at 8 p.m. on Monday between watching *Iron Chef* and *Masterpiece Mystery!*. Instead, they are choosing between watching *Iron Chef* then, or in a few hours with ad skipping on TiVo, or in a few days via $1.99 commercial-free download from iTunes, or on Hulu.com (which presents further choices about timeliness, availability, cost, and ad presence).

Media and information sectors feel the full and immediate brunt of information technology changes because the product itself consists of information. But the influence of technology—particularly cheap, plentiful bandwidth and communications—extends as well into physical products.

Consider the auto industry. Fifteen years ago, a consumer looking to buy her first car would walk into a dealership to ask questions and test-drive vehicles. Today's car consumer, in contrast, first goes to the Internet to do research on make, model, fuel efficiency, features, total cost of ownership, and price. Ninety percent of car buyers worldwide today conduct research on the Web before making a purchase.[6] Consumers now arrive at the dealer already knowing what they want to buy, what they should expect to pay, and what incentives the dealer has to close the sale. Such knowledge affords the dealer less flexibility to negotiate price or to upsell the undecided, and has been lowering the profit margin on sales of new cars. Hardly unique to the automobile industry, increased consumer ability to research, compare, and price shop any number of consumer items has created well-documented pricing pressure across almost all physical-goods markets.

Digitization has not only affected the purchase cycle of products. It has also changed the way a consumer uses and interacts with products. For cars, it used to be that the value was derived primarily from the vehicle's hardware: its look, speed, and comfort. But innovations in software and information delivery are increasingly shifting more of the functions that used to be left to the driver into the programmed systems managed by the car. In-car navigation and entertainment systems such as GM's OnStar,

Ford's Sync, and BMW's iDrive are adding more information and automation to the travel experience in the form of automatic climate control, radio settings, in-car GPS navigation, theft prevention, and other functions.[7] These changes may feel small today, but information is undoubtedly changing the experience on the road.

And what about products as nondigital as running shoes? A few years ago, a Nike product developer noticed more of his colleagues wearing ear buds on their lunch-hour runs. That observation led to a development partnership with Apple to create Nike+, a small insert that slips into the shoe and feeds data about the runner's pace and distance to her iPod. If she logs on to the Nike+ Web site, she can track her improvement over time and compare herself with friends, family, or other runners around the world. Suddenly, the value of the shoe no longer lies exclusively in the fit or the support. It lies in the information it can provide about performance. Nike+ running shoes are an early example of the "Internet of things"—more and more devices have the ability to gather and communicate information about what is happening around them.

The changes brought about by technology invite a shift away from demographic or psychographic segmentations into one that takes into account how consumers actually behave. When you can get information from running shoes and refrigerators, from cars and cribs, the limitation of relying on segments built on guesses about people's actual behaviors and desires becomes increasingly obvious. None of this suggests that consumer wants or tastes have disappeared. A consumer's tastes still dictate what products she seeks out and consumes. But what products and services the consumer wants tells sellers relatively little about the appropriate business model for delivering those products and services, and even less about the appropriate revenue model to drive the business model. In this case, the more important information is *how* the product is consumed. That analysis includes questions such as whether consumption is passive or active, in conjunction with other products or on its own, and the individual value received.

There are fairly famous (and useful) segmentations for the consumption of technology and tech-heavy products. Geoffrey Moore's *Crossing the Chasm* offers a simple and straightforward way for technology and electronics companies to place their target consumers into one of five segments: innovators, early adopters, early majority, late majority, and laggards.[8] Likewise, a simpler "ABC" approach used in B2B markets separates companies into early adopters, fast followers, and mainstream users.

Both of these approaches are useful, though they tend to work primarily for products that are expected to move linearly through the customer segments. In Moore's schema, a product can't really get to an early-majority member without first making it through the early adopters. These "comfort with technology" segmentations also largely assume that the product is used in more or less the same way across the various consumer categories.

One of the consequences of digitization and technological change is that products are *not* used in the same way across customer categories. Revenue innovation can take advantage of that variation by targeting different segments with different revenue models (the products may be exactly the same or packaged differently, which we'll address over the next few chapters).

Doing so requires more companies to adopt a segmentation based on how their customers interact with their products and how they use information as part of, or complementary to, the product or service itself. Since every industry is different, a segmentation approach that works in one may not work in another. In other words, there is no standard segmentation—it needs to be customized to each industry. But the basis of segmentation to drive revenue innovation is common across industries.

For the media and entertainment industry, my colleagues at IBM and I developed a segmentation on the basis of consumer product interaction and information use. This model has the most direct applicability to nonmedia industries with high or increasing information components, but the general approach applies to any industry. The IBM segmentation relies on three behavioral bases:

- Format of choice

- Consumption volume

- Degree of interaction

The format factor determines what form the product takes in what context. In media, format determines whether a consumer watches television programming on the TV set at home during prime-time hours, on a laptop while multitasking with e-mail or music, or on a portable device such as an iPhone—or some combination of the three. What is the dominant platform? How does platform choice change with time of day/week/year?

Consumption volume refers straightforwardly to how much of the product an individual consumes. In media, does the consumer watch, listen to, and read an average, above-average, or below-average amount? Does consumption volume fluctuate over the course of a day, week, or year?

Degree of interaction then asks whether an individual consumes a product passively or interacts and manipulates the content to suit his time and consumption preferences. Interaction also refers to the ability of service providers to pull information back from the customer about what he is consuming, when, and in what formats.

Massive Passives, Gadgetiers, Kool Kids: Segmentation in 3-D

The IBM Institute for Business Value, an internal think tank and research facility, has conducted an annual study since 2007 aimed at learning more about media consumers. When we analyze the ten thousand respondents according to their platform choices, consumption volumes, and formats, we uncover some interesting trends. For instance, 65 percent of people today still consume media primarily through their television set or stereo, while the remaining 35 percent have migrated to computers or handheld devices. Some consumers still consume standard shows with commercials, while others have abandoned prepackaged products in favor of mix-and-match options. These splits do have a generational element, though age is less relevant than technology use. On the basis of these factors, we saw three important behavioral consumer segments in media: the Massive Passives, the Gadgetiers, and the Kool Kids (see figure 1-1).

FIGURE 1–1

The digital divide: Massive Passives, Gadgetiers, and Kool Kids segment the media market

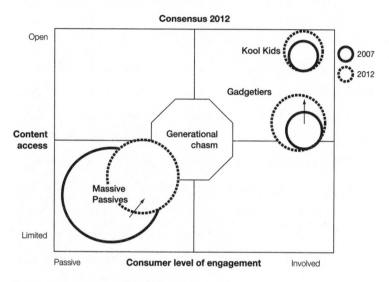

Source: IBM's Institute for Business Value.

Massive Passives

Massive Passives are traditional "one size fits all" consumers. They watch network television *on* a television while sitting in their living room. They are not active adopters of new technologies. If they own a TiVo or another digital video recorder (DVR) at all, it was most likely a gift or bundled with their cable subscription, and is hardly, if ever, used. This group is not usually motivated to customize their viewing experience, and they are happy to have their entertainment delivered to them in standard form.

Massive Passives are still, for now, the largest media consumer segment, making up 65 percent of all consumers. They have established brand loyalties, and their consumption accounts for the majority of revenues for the major media companies. While they are becoming more proactive in how they choose and consume media, the television will continue to be their device of choice.

Gadgetiers

In contrast to Massive Passives, Gadgetiers are active adopters of new technologies, making up around 15 percent of the consumer market. They balance their television watching with PC use and five or more other multimedia devices as well. Nothing is sacred. They will abandon that iPhone in a blink if they think some other device is better, cooler, or sleeker. You can tell a Gadgetier from the pile of briefly loved electronics stuffed in a box in their closets, each one abandoned for the next best thing. Gadgetiers tend to be more focused on time constraints, and so they are attracted to the time-shifting options afforded to them through devices such as the TiVo, or through downloadable television content available on the Web, and mobile content.

Gadgetiers are open to offerings that allow them to customize what they see and don't see; they're into components and playing around with new applications and self-styled bundles. They are often willing to pay more for advertisement-free content, as they are time sensitive. For media companies, Gadgetiers represent an opportunity for revenue generation outside of nontraditional sources and are a highly coveted group.

Kool Kids

The remaining 20 percent of consumers reside in a segment known as the Kool Kids, so named because they disproportionately overlap with younger generations. There is no one-to-one match, though; not all kids are Kids, and not all Kids are under twenty-four. In many ways, Kool Kids are more comfortable in front of a computer or a video game console than on an ottoman in front of the television, and they are highly skilled at customizing their media experience—what they watch, how they watch it, and when. They follow fads quickly, mix and match content streams into mash-ups, and create their own content—or at least consider what the industry calls "user-generated content" as equivalent to the slickly produced professional content that is the only thing consumed by Massive Passives. They actively trade music and video (shared and paid) either directly or over peer-to-peer networks.

Different Segments, Different Revenue Models

The advantage of the Massive Passives, Gadgetiers, and Kool Kids segmentation is that it allows companies to innovate revenue models for each segment. A product and revenue model must not always get through one group to reach another, as technologies must through Moore's innovators and early adopters. Many revenue models in fact will be successful largely because they concentrate on the interim needs of one segment for a specific period of time. For example, a number of booksellers in the United States and the United Kingdom have recently installed a device called the Espresso Book Machine, which prints paperback copies of books pulled from a catalog of licensed content. The Espresso feels like an innovation of the moment, relevant for this brief window while most Massive

Passive bibliophiles still prefer their books bound. In ten years, e-readers (e.g., Kindle) or tablet computers (e.g., iPad) will be the preferred Massive Passive reading platform, and the Espresso will be a producer of quaint nostalgia.

Which brings me to another point about behavioral segmentation: it can't be static. It is not meant to replace old ossified segmentation categories with new ossified segmentation categories. Instead, it is a dynamic segmentation, and the defining behaviors within each segment will shift as the behaviors that are new today become mainstream. Massive Passives today may consume most of their media from the television, but they also regularly use e-mail now, they are using social networking sites, and many now own smartphones, an unthinkable prospect just ten years ago. The Kids are also an ever-shifting group. Unlike the Gadgetiers, they are not true early adopters. Many of today's Kool Kids are simply following the crowd that surrounds them. Many, if not most, will transition to be the equivalent of Massive Passives.

The Massive Passives, Gadgetiers, and Kool Kids segmentation was designed for media and is immediately applicable to media and information sectors, as well as to the electronics and computer industries that provide the hardware on which media content is delivered. Yet there are segments like Massive Passives, Gadgetiers, and Kool Kids in other industries as well. Attitudes around the use of technology and information influence consumer buying decisions for many industries. I already mentioned a few ways this comes into play in the auto industry. Another current example is consumer utilities, where rising energy costs and increased awareness of climate change are driving consumers to be more proactive about energy consumption and power generation. Such proactive behavior is only possible because the product (electricity) is increasingly available in alternative formats (fossil fuels or renewables) and complemented with information about not just consumption volume (how much) but also consumption time patterns (peak or off-peak). These dynamics are giving Gadgetier-like consumers greater ability to adjust and customize. These changes are already driving a shift in the unit-cost revenue model that dominates the sector, and there's tremendous opportunity for revenue innovation based on behavioral consumer segments.

Behavioral segments like Massive Passives, Gadgetiers, and Kool Kids can be applied usefully today to industries including automotive and utilities, of course, but also financial services, health care, education, travel, and gambling. These sectors share the following characteristics:

- Either the product consists of information, or information plays an increasing role in the value delivered to consumers.

- Technology is creating rapid change in the industry.

- Product functionality is changing rapidly.

- There is potential to pull information back from the user.

I am not making an argument in favor of the specific digital consumer segmentation I helped design. Instead, the key point is the urgency of adding behavioral bases to whatever segmentation schema you are currently using. These behavioral bases will point the path to revenue innovation opportunities.

Once a firm understands its behavioral segments, it will then be able to develop separate revenue models for those segments, and innovate those models on an ongoing basis. This will not be easy to do. Most companies when asked to find new revenue sources automatically think of new products. This is true across all industries. IBM's CEO studies show repeatedly that companies are more likely to innovate with new or upgraded products than through any other approach. It's somehow engrained in the corporate DNA and very difficult to change.[9]

In media, this tendency means that content creators often approach innovation by coming up with a new game or a new show or a new movie or a new artist, which they package and deliver in the same way they always have with the same pricing model on the same platform used by the majority of customers. This becomes a problem when a company has a product loved by customers who are not using traditional platforms.

Consider what happened to NBC when comedian Conan O'Brien failed to achieve the same audience levels and ratings for the *Tonight Show* as former host Jay Leno had enjoyed. After seven months with O'Brien at the helm, NBC opted to give Leno his old 11:35 p.m. slot back.

On the surface this looks like a simple advertising equation—Leno could deliver higher impressions, so he earned the better slot. But shift platforms, and there was a veritable outpouring of support for O'Brien on the social media sites Facebook and Twitter.[10] NBC knew going into it that O'Brien's audience was younger than Leno's.[11] But the support for O'Brien shown by digital audiences suggests that the problem is not only demographic, it is behavioral—a bulk of O'Brien's audience simply wasn't consuming programming from the television any-more.

Yet most consumers still do watch television, which brings forth a second reason why revenue innovation targeted to specific behavior segments will require a new mind-set for most companies. Namely, executives look at their dominant audience base and find it difficult to understand why they should take on the risk and expense of developing new models for minority segments when most of their current revenue and profit comes from a core customer base. They only realize their mistake when it is too late—after a competitor or new entrant has innovated a profitable way to take on the smaller segments and eat into the main revenue base of the industry. That's the story of the media industry over the last decade.

A case in point: as recently as 2006, the music industry earned 90 percent of its revenues from sales of physical CDs. A music industry exec would have looked at that point in time at his core customer base and revenue source and reasonably rejected any proposal that might have put that revenue stream at risk. But in 2010, physical CD sales in the United States will account for only 50 percent of revenues.[12] Worldwide, it will take a few more years for digital music revenues to come to parity with CD sales, but the point is that this is a one-way train. Just four years, and the dominant revenue model in the music industry is becoming a niche due to the combined effects of digitization of content, consumer Internet use, technology change, and changing consumer behavior.

Something similar happened in video rental. As we saw in the case that opened this chapter, Netflix took 36 percent market share from the retail rental chains in just a few years of business. It did not gain its initial traction by changing the core product. The company still delivered physical DVDs. Now that digitization is more firmly under way, Netflix offers delivery on demand of streamed film and television content, which by some interpretations is a shift in the product. But Netflix innovated first around the revenue and business model before it embraced innovation around the product. The customer segment had to be ready, which, given that Amazon too launched a streaming video on demand service in 2010, it appears now to be.

Like many incumbent media companies, Blockbuster, the music labels, and a number of other players were at a disadvantage to new entrants when it came to identifying customer behavioral segments and creating strategies for them. That behavioral segmentation that new players seem so good at is a prerequisite for revenue innovation—none of what comes in the following chapters is possible without first understanding changing, and more fine-grained, consumer preferences and consumption patterns.

The New Segmentation in Media

So what might have changed for media players if they had been looking at their consumer base via behavioral segments? In 2008, music labels and retailers earned annual revenues that totaled a mere 60 percent of what they'd tallied at the high point of music sales in 2000.[13] The shift to digital formats for music had certainly opened the door to a great deal of music piracy and peer-to-peer sharing by Kool Kids, but the piracy story has been oversold as an explanation for revenue declines. The majority of those music revenues shifted somewhere else— partly to iTunes, which saw that the Gadgetiers would buy lots of individual songs rather than whole albums, and to tickets for live shows.

The music labels did not see the nuances of the shift while it was happening. They saw that revenues were in decline, but since 90 percent of 2006 revenues still came from CDs, they attributed the revenue losses to the behavior of some fringe consumers—pirates and members of peer-to-peer networks, such as the original Napster. The behavior of the more mainstream Gadgetiers completely slipped below the radar.

The early response of the music labels and their brick-and-mortar retail distributors was to protect CD sales, rather than respond with a commercial offer that allowed for the sale of whole digital albums as well as songs. This resistance wasn't new. Back in 1986, I was an adviser to a start-up called Personics that attempted something like an analog iTunes. The company put machines in record stores that would allow customers to make, and pay for, custom mixtapes of exactly the sort that most teenagers were busy making for free at home. Personics didn't survive for a variety of reasons, including the cost and complexity of the extant technology in 1986. But the biggest issue by far was the music labels' refusal to allow Personics access to enough of their catalogs to make the offer appealing to customers. Even then the music labels lost the opportunity to innovate a new revenue stream and control the terms while they were still in a position of power.

Fast-forward twenty years and the music labels were "blindsided" when digitization allowed customers to do the same mixing and swapping of songs they always had, except much more efficiently and at much greater volume. In a panic now that technology had finally shifted the power dynamics in the music industry, the music labels sued the peer-to-peer networks, particularly the original Napster, in the hopes of stopping the swell of piracy and music swapping. And they blindly negotiated a deal with iTunes that allowed Apple's online music retailer to sell whole albums at $9.99 and individual songs for $0.99 a piece, the latter at a less-than-advantageous revenue split.

For its part, Apple didn't need to make money from music. It just needed to have music available to fill out its one-stop model of easy-to-use hardware, software, and cataloging. A similar dynamic applied to cellular service providers and ringtones, for which the labels received an even less advantageous 50 percent split on a $2.50-for-a-snippet revenue model.

If the music labels had seen the reality of segmentation in their market, they could have developed cooperative commercial models geared toward Gadgetiers and Kool Kids. Such a strategy would have given the labels, rather than iTunes, the dominant interface with the customer. For the Gadgetiers, the labels could have developed an à la carte pricing model that allowed Gadgetiers to easily buy individual songs rather than whole albums. By doing it themselves, they could arguably have set the single-song price point higher than where iTunes ultimately landed. Maybe they could have even come up with the variable pricing model that iTunes has now adopted, with different prices assigned to different songs based on popularity.

This is not just twenty-twenty hindsight. Two researchers from The Wharton School of the University of Pennsylvania showed that the price per song that consumers are willing to theoretically pay is markedly higher than $0.99. In their study, five hundred Penn undergraduates in the fall of 2008 were asked to listen to the iTunes fifty most popular songs and write down the most they would be willing to pay for each. The study was repeated early in 2009. The results show that if every song were given the same price tag, the uniform price that the sample consumers were willing to pay was $2.30 in 2008 and $1.49 in 2009.[14]

That research, though conducted only with a small subset of the population that perhaps fits into just one of the behavioral segments, shows what might have happened had the music labels and retailers been willing to embrace the changes brought about by technology and consumer expectation trends, and created a model targeted to the consumption patterns of Gadgetiers. As for the Kool Kids, segmentation may have allowed the music labels to see that attacking the peer-to-peer networks was an exercise in futility. For every entity like the original Napster, there are hundreds of private peer-to-peer exchanges or music-posting blogs run by enthusiasts who keep the networks invitation-only. Kool Kids don't see music exchange as stealing any more than teenagers a generation ago thought there was anything wrong with making tape copies to give to friends. Every ounce of energy and money devoted to prosecuting this behavior could have been directed at potentially profitable revenue innovation. For example, the labels might have given Kool Kids music for free in exchange for revenues from other pieces of the value chain: concert ticket sales, for example, or merchandise branded to the musician, or even a cut of hardware sales.[15]

New Revenue Opportunities in Media

Music labels are finally responding to the opportunities presented by a new segmentation. One approach they are pursuing involves looking at the complete music value chain, from recordings to concerts to merchandise. Their road is long, though, since everyone from cell phone service providers to concert promoters to Walmart is trying the same thing.

Some new possibilities are emerging in *windowing* as well—windowing refers to the revenue window that media companies enjoy when a product is released in its highest-price form (a film in theaters, for example) and before it is available through other platforms, such as video. Digitization has shortened those windows significantly, but they still exist and can be used to drive revenue. For example, a VIP-video service by film distributors aimed at high-volume Gadgetiers could charge a premium subscription for streamed versions of brand-new releases that are not yet available from the rental retailers. Or a television-oriented Web site such as ZillionTV could release new shows "fully loaded" with advertising, and then remove ads and move to unit sales as the show gets older.

Digitization and windowing also present options for reversing the traditional revenue models for the "best" customers. Typically, the most loyal customers are rewarded for their volume and consistency with discounted offers. But it may in fact be that the customers who use the most product are the ones most willing to pay for it. Metered models adopted by online versions of newspapers like the *Financial Times* or "freemium" models I talk about in the pricing chapter both assume that the more you consume, the more you will pay.

Overall, the lesson from music is that digitization will drive behavioral changes within certain segments of customers—it is truly unavoidable. It is smart and necessary to protect existing revenue streams, but it is also necessary to create separate business models for the segments that behave differently. In the media industry, the three segments require three approaches, and those approaches can't be static. We're no longer moving from one market steady state to another, with just a brief period of upheaval. Technology is changing rapidly along with customer experiences and expectations. In response, the models that best address customer need and willingness to pay will need to adapt continuously.

Learning from the Media Industry

As examples of how other industries can learn from the media industry's struggles, let's look again at consumer utilities and automobiles, as well as casinos and grocery retailers. Specifically, let's examine how segmentation along the lines of the Massive Passives, Gadgetiers, and Kool Kids applies to a few of these sectors, and how sectors with different bases are developing behavioral segmentations of their own.

The utilities arm of IBM's Institute for Business Value has uncovered four profiles in consumer utilities that are analogous to the Massive Passives, Gadgetiers, and Kool Kids segments for media, shown in figure 1-2. The trends driving these behaviors in the utilities sector include rising energy costs, desire for more control and choice than traditional providers have given, and awareness of climate change, among others.

FIGURE 1-2

Utility industry segmentation model

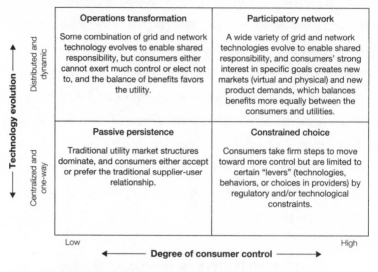

		Low ← Degree of consumer control → High	
Technology evolution ↑↓	**Distributed and dynamic**	**Operations transformation** Some combination of grid and network technology evolves to enable shared responsibility, but consumers either cannot exert much control or elect not to, and the balance of benefits favors the utility.	**Participatory network** A wide variety of grid and network technologies evolve to enable shared responsibility, and consumers' strong interest in specific goals creates new markets (virtual and physical) and new product demands, which balances benefits more equally between the consumers and utilities.
	Centralized and one-way	**Passive persistence** Traditional utility market structures dominate, and consumers either accept or prefer the traditional supplier-user relationship.	**Constrained choice** Consumers take firm steps to move toward more control but are limited to certain "levers" (technologies, behaviors, or choices in providers) by regulatory and/or technological constraints.

Source: IBM's Institute for Business Value.

The utility behavioral profiles can be mapped in a matrix with a horizontal axis measuring the decision maker's willingness to take control over his energy options and the vertical axis representing the technological changes currently taking place in the way energy is delivered. Those that have been willing and able to take advantage of "smart" metering technology and distributed energy generation—mostly people with high income—are considered "energy stalwarts," the Gadgetiers of the consumer utilities market. These folks are investing disposable income in technologies such as off-grid solar or wind power–generating technologies (see figure 1-2).

The upper left-hand corner belongs to the "frugal goal seeker," electricity's Kool Kids. They don't have the money for expensive, technical solutions, or they don't feel like spending the money they have on them, so will seek less expensive, innovative alternatives to controlling their energy usage. In the lower left- and right-hand corners reside the "passive rate payer" and the "energy epicure," the industry's Massive Passives. These segments are resistant to change, be it due to inertia or inattention, in the case of the passive rate payers, or a desire for unlimited power regardless of cost, in the case of the epicures.

For the utilities providers, these customer profiles offer opportunities to innovate the traditional unit-based utilities revenue model. Experiments in the use of smart meters have shown that better information can influence consumers to use energy differently, so energy providers might be able to create a variable pricing model, whereby customers could be charged a lower price for energy consumed during off-peak periods. Utilities thought leaders also imagine a future of "smart homes," which link electronics in the home to a centralized information system managed by the user. Such a system could allow dad to make sure he did indeed turn off the iron before he left for the office, or let mom view the inventory of the family refrigerator from her phone in the grocery store, all priced within a broader service model.

Segmentation in Atoms Industries

The energy company of the future will rely heavily on two-way communication between the consumer and the provider about consumption patterns. But what about atoms-based industries in which communication traditionally stops at the point of sale? The new behavioral segmentation applies there too.

Like media, automotive has long employed age-and-sex-driven segmentations to determine what cars to develop and market: sports cars for the testosterone-driven male, minivans or hatchbacks for soccer moms. And you really can get any color you want. There was only one way to make money from those cars, though: sell or lease them.

A Massive Passives, Gadgetiers, and Kool Kids view of the auto industry presents some alternative possibilities. Massive Passive drivers will stick with traditional platforms for now, so they will continue to invest in fossil fuel–run vehicles for the time being. Gadgetiers will probably also buy cars, but they may be drawn to models with significant technology upgrades, such as heads-up displays and sophisticated computerized control systems. To appeal to Gadgetiers, such features have to allow the user to take control—Gadgetiers like playing with technology, not just using it. One relatively recent example of a misreading of the technology behavior of Massive Passives and Gadgetiers is BMW's introduction of iDrive in 2001. The explicit rationale for the system was to simplify a range of complex physical controls for such features as climate control and the audio and navigation systems by merging them into a single electronic interface. The execution was off, though. BMW designed a system as sophisticated as its cars, but it was so complex that Massive Passive–type drivers could not figure out how to use it, while Gadgetiers were frustrated because the system didn't allow much customization. No one was happy until BMW dramatically revamped the iDrive, both to make it more user friendly and to allow more customization.

As an alternative to car ownership, Gadgetiers may also be attracted to automotive models such as the one offered by Better

Place, the electric automotive start-up launched by former SAP executive Shai Agassi. Agassi believes that for electric cars to make a real difference to emissions levels, they must be adopted by the majority of drivers. One way to do that is for Better Place to completely change the revenue model. Instead of selling cars for a price that covers manufacturing and yields a profit, Better Place makes the purchase price very low—basically at the cost of a year's worth of gas—while the company keeps ownership of the batteries so the company earns service revenue on miles driven and battery charging or switching.[16]

Kool Kids may bypass car ownership altogether. They'll ride the train or alter their ride by day or mood with car sharing via companies like Zipcar. Zipcar is the largest car-sharing company in the United States. Its model allows urban drivers to reserve a car for between one hour and four days and pay a usage fee (fuel and insurance included). (See table 1-1.)

Segmentation in Casinos: A Behavioral Approach

The examples from utilities and automotive show how a Massive Passives, Gadgetiers, and Kool Kids–like segmentation can function in some atoms industries. This model is not useful for everyone, though, particularly not for atoms or service sectors whose products are little augmented by information and technology. In those cases, a behavioral segmentation that employs bases relevant to the specific industry will be needed.

Let's look at how the casino business is tackling this challenge. Casinos have been using segmentation models for a long time in order to concentrate their promotions and free rooms

TABLE 1-1

Segmentation in brief

	Massive Passives	Gadgetiers	Kool Kids
Profile	Skews older	Early adopters	The under-24 segment
Media consumption habits	• Passive "lean back" experience • Traditional media as centerpiece (e.g., TV, printed newspaper, DVD)	• Heavily involved experience • TV, PC, and mobile equal use	• Heavily involved and integrated social experiences • Mobile as centerpiece
Device adoption	Device laggards	Device leaders	Device aspirants
Degree of control	• Scheduled programs • Some DVR time-shifting	• Prevalent time-shifting • Place-shifting with PC, devices	• Prevalent time-shifting • Place-shifting with mobile, physical copies
Primary innovation approach	• Pricing innovation • Prepackaged bundles	• Packaging innovation • Self-styled experience	• Payer innovation • P2P, or third-party supported (e.g., free)
Monetization goal	Revenue maintenance	Revenue growth	Revenue cultivation

on the gamers who lose more than they win. In the early years of segmentation in the casino industry, companies relied on a kind of geographic/demographic profile based on why the customer was there. Was it a convention? A packaged tour? Was the customer a private or invited guest? How far did the customer travel to get there? Such information gave the casino some insight into what the customer likely wanted to do during the visit, and helped drive promotions.

Increased competition forced some casinos to become more nuanced. A few players now look more closely toward behavioral bases to find out not only what customers *do* while at the casino (What games do they play? How much do they spend? Where do they eat? What do they drink? What nongambling activities do they engage in?), but also *how* they do it (Do they gamble socially with a friend or spouse or alone? Do they call attention to themselves, or do they prefer to stay quiet and anonymous?).

This information has resulted in a behavioral segmentation used by some firms in the casino industry to divide players into five unequal segments: *recognition seekers*, who want freebies and top service from the locale; *escapists*, who just want to play and be left alone; *reward seekers*, who frequent locales because they are members of the rewards programs; *socializers*, who develop strong loyalty to a locale and its personnel and go there for the social aspect of the place; and *professionals*, who want to make money and manipulate the system.[17] Casinos have developed different approaches for how they market to these segments to keep the unprofitable professionals away and the highly profitable socializers coming.

Harrah's is considered a leader in the use of behavioral segmentation in the casino industry, and it is going even further in using behavioral data to segment customers. Its approach relies on a loyalty program called Total Rewards. Customers insert magnetic cards into slot machines and other games, and the system tracks their activity. Customers accumulate points based on how much they spend, and the system analyzes and cross-references the customer information in order to predict what kind of rewards might most appeal to this customer and keep him or her coming back. Instead of relying on the manager's best guess, Total Rewards figures out what kind of customer it has, who is the most profitable, and what that customer needs to return to a Harrah's location sooner than she might have otherwise.[18]

Segmentation Differentiates Grocery Chains

Some grocers have also begun analyzing behavioral data collected on loyalty-type cards as a basis for customer segmentation initiatives. This approach is a shift away from a decades-old reliance on geography and demographics to determine the inventory mix, the type of promotions to place in weekly circulars, and the socioeconomic market to pursue. In the mid-1990s in the United Kingdom, for instance, the fight for dominance was being waged between Marks & Spencer and Sainsbury's high-end grocery stores, known for their rows of bright produce and prepared meals. Asda stores competed for the price-sensitive customer with rock-bottom prices. In this constellation, Tesco might have been an also-ran.

But Tesco broke out of the dominant socioeconomic segmentation when it launched its Clubcard rewards program. Shoppers signed up with a name and address, and swiped the card for discounts every time they shopped. Tesco's system captured the behavioral purchase data and identified the products the customer bought frequently. This information determined what coupons Tesco sent uniquely to the customer in a monthly mailing meant to entice them back to the store. The relevance of those offers was far more effective than one-size-fits-all promotions. The industry average for coupon use is between 1 and 2 percent, but Clubcard members used their coupons 20 percent of the time.

Tesco has used its Clubcard data more strategically as well. For instance, when Walmart bought Asda, Tesco searched its database to identify the customers who consistently opted for the lowest-priced item in a category. It then lowered the prices on the products those customers purchased most often. As a result, the customer defections that many anticipated in the first months of the Asda acquisition did not happen. Likewise, when Tesco wanted to jettison a low-selling brand of Polish bread in one of its branches, Clubcard data revealed that the neighborhood's Polish community *only* went to Tesco because it carried it. Rather than ditch the bread, Tesco added a brand of kielbasa popular in Poland, along with a slew of other attractive items. Sales in that store grew apace.[19]

Tesco's approach is different because its use of data is going straight to the behavior—what are people buying—and correlating those purchase behaviors with other behaviors and better offers. Certainly, neighborhood and store and even socioeconomics play a role, but Tesco is not relying on these details and correlating to the possible behaviors. It is instead looking at the behaviors and catering directly to them.

The current economic crisis has made price sensitivity a larger factor than before, and recent announcements show that Tesco is revamping its Clubcard program as a result of decreased effectiveness. Tesco has also been joined in its approach by other competitors. For instance, Sam's Club in the United States has started fine-tuning its discounts based on customer purchase patterns in a manner similar to Tesco's. Limited to "eValues Plus" card members who pay a higher annual membership fee, the Sam's Club model delivers customized coupons to shoppers based on the products they buy most often. The result is that two customers might pay a dramatically different price for the same product, depending on their prior behavior. As with Tesco, Sam's Club reports that 20 to 30 percent of issued coupons get used.[20]

Segmentation Pitfalls

I hear two frequent concerns about the behavioral segmentation we developed in the media industry, concerns that apply to any behavioral segmentation. The first is that this approach yields segments that are too broad. At a time when marketing experts are talking about "audiences of one," dividing the world into three or four unequal parts seems unsophisticated.

That assessment is dead-on—companies *should* be thinking about delivering a unique experience for each customer, especially those companies whose products are digital and therefore cheap to alter and deliver. A three-way segmentation like Massive Passives, Gadgetiers, and Kool Kids defines only the *first level* at which companies need to segment. Only once a high-level set of behavioral categories are identified can companies then drill down to personalize the product or service.

But remember that this book is about revenue innovation, not product innovation. It is unlikely and unnecessary for companies to create a separate revenue model for each individual customer. The higher-level behavioral segmentation we created for media is the right level at which to apply revenue model opportunities. The products that then flow through that model can be further personalized as customer wants dictate.

A second, entirely contrary objection is that a behavioral segmentation is too fine. Executives rightly ask why they should do anything for the Gadgetiers and Kool Kids given the size of the

Massive Passive market. In media, for every person who has abandoned his television for a laptop, millions more still *want* to be home at eight o'clock on a Wednesday night. It is hard to convince an executive of the need for change when his company still makes millions from a dominant user base.

All industry incumbents fear cannibalizing their existing revenues through new revenue model innovations. Consumers do not divide themselves evenly across segments. No matter what industry you are in, the bulk of your revenues is likely to come from one or two customer segments, so it is not illogical to ponder whether innovation will endanger current revenue streams.

Yet this perspective misinterprets the nature of the risk. Executives who worry about disrupting their dominant revenue streams are often operating under a tacit belief that revenues are safe so long as the company doesn't change anything. Put another way, it assumes that customers aren't changing. This assumption is wrong. Customers are changing, and competitors, old and new, are offering innovative revenue models. Delaying innovation in order to protect current revenue streams is simply capitulation to the faster-moving competition.

There is a way to go that is less risky to dominant segments but still gets you the experience you need to move: innovate new revenue models for the smaller segments, particularly those that show greater use of information or digitization and are doing more interacting and manipulation of the product. In addition to potential revenue gains, these experiments have an important benefit: they allow you to gain experience and have a working revenue model for when the larger segments start to shift behavior. Wait until they are gone, and you will find it pretty tough to win them back without a new innovation or dramatically better value proposition. You can't just copy innovators after the fact. Consider that Blockbuster launched a mail-based rental service to compete with Netflix and even priced it slightly lower, but it seems to have topped out in 2006 at 3 million subscribers, with dramatic reductions in the years since. Meanwhile, Netflix trucks along with a robust 10 million subscribers and growing.[21]

Even worse, Blockbuster is now losing ground among its core Massive Passives. Its focus on holding Passives in the retail stores and recapturing defected Gadgetiers caused it to miss the next shift in capturing the Massive Passive customer. Launched by Redbox, this new model exploded beginning in 2007 with a $1-a-day movie rental model delivered via stand-alone kiosks in high-traffic retail environments like grocery stores and pharmacies. By 2009, kiosk rental had captured 19 percent of the video market, mostly at the expense of brick-and-mortar rental.[22] Reacting, Blockbuster now has a kiosk model of its own, at the same time that it is stocking retail locations with snacks, drinks, electronics, and other accessories to movie watching in an effort to lure Massive Passives into the store.[23]

Similar missed opportunities abound in media, illustrating why it is so urgent to begin behavioral segmentation and innovate revenue models. Incumbents struggle to come up with ways to address the new behaviors in their markets while still protecting traditional revenue flows. This impulse is not entirely foolish. It is important to keep current customers buying. Yet it is equally important to not overestimate their buying power. Your largest segment may include the majority of your revenue, but it may not include the most intensive buyers. The president of Sony Music Entertainment's Global Digital Business, Thomas Hesse, touched on this in late 2009 at the *Economist* Media Convergence Forum when he said that 50 percent of Sony's music revenues come from digital sources, derived from only 15 percent of the company's customers.

If you stick to traditional correlation-based demographic or VALS segmentation and keep your eyes on the biggest chunk of the existing revenue stream, you are going to miss the shifts and opportunities that will allow you to grow. When these shifts start affecting that large static segment you've been focused on, the price points, value streams, and revenue sources will have already been set by competitors.

The third issue with behavioral segmentation is that most companies will simply find it very difficult to do. Identifying customer segments and creating a valuable personalized experience requires a great deal of accurate, well-analyzed data that has traditionally been difficult to collect and even more difficult to interpret.

Some consolation should come from the fact that segmentation in the digital age makes personalization easier. Some might even say that the dominant technology trends of low-cost communications and low-cost bandwidth have made personalization *possible*. Before digitization, the products and information really only flowed one-way, from producers to consumers. There was no easy way to pull information back, to interact individually with customers or gauge likes and tendencies. In the media industry in particular, so much consumption is a shared experience anyway—the family watches television together, or a couple goes out for a movie—that individual tastes do not always translate into individual consumption.

There is a two-way flow of information now, as companies push products and consumers leave a trail of data behind them that shows what they consume or buy. In the media industry, the tools were there to enable a behavioral segmentation long before they were used. The cable set-top box can see what played on the television, for how long, and when people switched; the IP address can identify what people clicked on, how long they stayed, and what they eventually purchased. Rating tools, comment pages, and social media allow customers to provide direct feedback. Traditional media is now beginning to collect this data and analyze it to better develop segment-oriented packages or pricing models.

The possibilities here are exciting, though I do not want to undersell the challenge. Companies that have done the most in this area are almost unanimous in their opinion that collecting reliable data and storing it for useful analysis and application is a big headache. Most data today identifies what customers have already done, not what they plan to do. Predictive analytics have been largely hit or miss, and expensive to boot. As a result, nobody really knows with any certainty what customers are going to be willing to spend their time and money consuming—not even the consumer herself. In my view, such uncertainty means opportunity for those who can get started early and learn through experimentation. There are no shortcuts.

There's also the large question of building and maintaining trust with users so that you are allowed to collect the behavioral data you need. Much of what I'm talking about is nonpersonal data and certainly doesn't rise to the level of company secrets. Thus far most people don't seem to be overly concerned that Apple knows what songs they listen to, or Nike knows how often they run and how far. But everyone does expect to receive some value in exchange for giving value (at least to for-profit companies), and everyone expects to be treated with respect and dignity. Companies that gather and use information on behavior in ways that even appear unseemly could shut themselves out of the ability to gather data for a long time and put themselves at a huge competitive disadvantage.

Segmentation Lessons

There are a number of lessons I see from the media's experimentation (or lack thereof) with new segmentation. Stories from the home video and music industries illustrate the risk of continuing to only watch the behavior of the dominant segment—they cannot tell you what is coming. In the media industry, while the Massive Passives sit in the living room, Gadgetiers and Kool Kids are using new technologies and new product delivery, working out the bugs and kinks. The experiments that are not worthwhile die on the vine. Those that can survive take hold and go mainstream, right into the living room, where the Massive Passives adopt them.

And Massive Passives will adopt them. The revenue from the Passive segment is not safe forever. IBM Digital Consumer Survey data shows that Massive Passives today are more technology savvy than they were just a few years ago. In five years, Passives will be savvier still. By experimenting with segment-specific models today, companies give themselves an opportunity to identify what is working and what could work better. They set themselves a place at the negotiating table, where they can help shape the market's pricing and terms.

More sophisticated segmentation based on behavioral data gathered back from customers allows companies to develop some creative revenue models and experiment with them on a portion of customers who are already open to change—and by extension, already at risk. For example, a year from now, the *Wall Street Journal* may charge a premium to deliver "early bird" content at 11 p.m. to a Gadgetier's BlackBerry; it may keep the standard subscription for a Massive Passive who wants the paper on his door; and it could seek some digital ad support to monetize Kool Kid tweets that reference *WSJ*. These three approaches to the same content will coexist.

Once behavioral segment–based revenue models are in place, companies will be in a better position to track how customers use products and services in order to identify tastes and preferences that bring offerings down to the level of *personalization*—that market of one. Returning to our highly likely hypothetical about the *WSJ*, the News Corporation surely knows that its 11 p.m. digital delivery is an option that only a Gadgetier could love, since the Massive Passive can't get past the complexity, and the Kool Kid spends those hours out with friends. But does every Gadgetier want *all* the content? A financial exec may want to know just about the markets; a twentysomething professional may want just Life & Style on Fridays, whereas a marketing exec may opt for a greater mix. Digitization of content makes all of these content mixes possible. Only experience and experiments will make clear the best mix of pricing and content.

The "best mix" will change frequently as new technologies emerge and customer expectations evolve. So remember to gather feedback from your various segment-focused revenue innovations and integrate ideas that make the experience better.

It Gets Better with Time

Fortunately, the technology systems that collect and analyze information over the Web are designed to get better the more they are used. Take Amazon.com as a case in point. In 1998, the recommendations Amazon's engine produced were truly bizarre. For years, an acquaintance of mine had to glance past ads for the novels of Gabriel Garcia Marquez, all because she once ordered a book for a daughter taking an undergrad course in magical realism. Amazon's recommendations today are much closer to the mark because experience has led to improvements that better filter anomalous purchases from more enduring tastes.

Google's search engine probably does the best job at producing relevant, in-the-moment information, which is one of the reasons why Google continues to dominate the search business. Such success is then self-perpetuating: the more customers tell Google or Amazon what they like—whether by clicking or buying—the more data the tools have to make informed selections and recommendations. This approach is catching on on the Web, evident everywhere from Netflix to Pandora.

Web 2.0 technologies offer still another way to understand the views of the customer. Akin to the uncensored reviews, corporate social media efforts such as Facebook pages offer a window into the customer's attitudes toward a product, as GM found recently when its Tahoe social media campaign was hijacked by some creative environmentalists whose videos lampooned the Tahoe's gas-guzzling and found a large audience on YouTube.

Almost everyone viewed the Tahoe debacle as a misstep. And yet GM gained the opportunity to engage a part of the audience it would not have access to otherwise. I am not talking about the environmentalist community—its members are not going to be in the market for an SUV anytime soon. Instead, I am talking about average drivers who like the form, safety, and design of the SUV, but are concerned about the environmental issues. The company builds awareness of GM through such efforts and creates a forum for concerned consumers to tell the company what they think.

The technology orientation of many of these examples—Amazon, Google, social media—should not be taken to mean that the lessons learned from experiments in segmentation have no bearing on the Massive Passives. They do. Remember that some efforts that survive the scrutiny of the Gadgetiers and Kool Kids will find their way to the Massive Passives. If they are good enough, they may even pull the Massive Passives into the digital age more rapidly.

For instance, digital consumers of Blockbuster's online rental service can receive on-the-fly recommendations based on a rental history, but Blockbuster can also take what it learns about customer likes and dislikes to the retail store and use it to drive store displays that connect unlikely inventory. Retail outlets can also collect rental data through its retail point-of-sale systems. The personalization may not be in-the-moment, but it is a start.

Examples and inspiration can come from many industries—both in the brick-and-mortar world and online. Retail financial services have been experimenting with data to drive segmentation and personalization for well over a decade. Such data may allow a bank to offer a home equity loan to customers whose credit card transactions show surges in spending on home improvement items. Or an automotive salesman may structure a public school teacher's financing to her ten-month income schedule. These possibilities are compelling, and they only present themselves once a company identifies its segments.

Getting Started

For companies that want to pursue revenue innovation, how should they integrate more sophisticated behavioral segmentation? Revenue innovation requires change in strategy, operations, and infrastructure. You need to assess for each whether you have the skills and capabilities in place to execute. For segmentation, you should ask the following questions.

Strategy

- Do you have a clear understanding of your consumer segments and their characteristics?

- Do you understand their product, channel, and revenue model preferences and how they interact with your brands?

- Do you have a differentiated strategy for driving incremental revenues from the various consumer segments?

- Do you have a sense of the current and potential value derived from each segment?

Infrastructure

- Is your infrastructure flexible and scalable to evolve with your customers as they shift their behavior?

- Do you have the ability to share costs and develop scale to serve smaller segments?

- Do your systems enable you to track consumer behavior across digital channels?

Operations

- Do you have established processes in place to segment your consumer base, and act on the segmentation?

- Is your organization aligned to focus on the consumer across products, geographies, and channels?

- Is your operating model flexible enough to allow both profitable scaling for large segments and profitable customization for small segments?

2

Pricing Innovation

The prom king has always been able to rent a tuxedo for "the big event." But what about the queen? Her choices are mostly limited to wearing something she already owns, borrowing from a friend, or buying an expensive new dress—imperfect options for the fashion-forward on a budget. No young woman wants to wear "this old thing" for a special event. A borrowed dress may not offer the best style-match or fit, and new dresses, as all parents of daughters know, can be shockingly expensive. And don't forget that she still needs accessories.

Fashion start-up Rent the Runway has hit on a solution: fashion rental. Started by two newly minted MBAs who obviously learned something about business models, the new venture buys inventory from top designers and then rents it to customers for four-day blocks at a cost of between $50 and $200 per dress—low enough that a young woman could effectively rent all the dresses she needs for a season at the same price it would have cost her to buy a single dress.

Worried about fit? Rent the Runway posts detailed sizing information, has a staff of stylists available via phone or chat to provide advice, and will ship two sizes at no extra cost, just to be sure. It also adds a "fit kit" of double-sided tape and bra adjusters so the renter can prevent bunching and puckering. By using a beta-test model and friends-and-family networking, the company had twenty-thousand members at its launch in November 2009.[1]

What to Pay? When to Pay It?

Rent the Runway is an example of *pricing innovation*, the first of the three revenue innovation approaches we'll examine. Pricing innovation involves rethinking the pricing model for a given product—in terms of both the amount of money charged and the point (or points) in time when the customer is required to pay. The pricing models outlined in this chapter include subscriptions, variable pricing, pricing by parts, à la carte and bundled pricing, and rentals. See figure 2-1 for an overview of pricing innovation models. These models by themselves are familiar—we've all used them at some point. The innovation comes from applying pricing structures atypical to the relevant industry, as Rent the Runway is doing by offering a rental model within retail fashion, a typical sell-through industry.

A big part of pricing innovation comes from experimenting with different pricing models for the same product, angled to appeal to different consumer segments. Pricing innovations can

FIGURE 2-1

Pricing innovation models

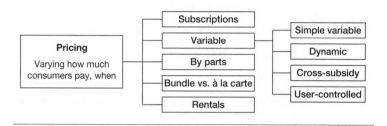

also be mixed and matched with payer and package innovations (discussed in the following chapters), as needed.

To date there haven't been many experiments with mixed pricing models to target different customer segments. I suspect it's because pricing innovation activates fears of cannibalization, and so many companies shy away from it. Nonetheless, there is still plenty to learn from the pricing innovations that are taking place in media and in other industries, and there is plenty of room for more experimentation still to come.

Payer Attitudes Toward Price

Will customers pay? has always been one of the defining questions of a business model—and one that has tripped up many an immaculate business plan. The question seems to have taken on a new urgency in the digital age. But the idea that people won't pay for digital products is largely overblown—the situation has never been as dire as many pundits have made it out to be, even in the media industry. Contrary to the current debate around free content, most customers do pay for digital products. More still would pay if the pricing structure effectively took into account usage volumes, device preferences, location, and other factors relevant to the digital consumer. So the more relevant question for pricing innovators is *how* will customers pay?

Willingness to pay is a funny thing. Sometimes it is tied to how a consumer has been trained to think about a product. For instance, banking customers are often given no-charge access to their accounts through ATMs, phone, and the Internet in exchange for maintaining a minimum balance. That balance means the account holder is, in fact, "paying" for his account with interest the bank has earned from lending deposit money to others. But the customer doesn't see that. He thinks phone service and visits to the branch are free. Such misconceptions between the cost of delivering a product and service and the "price"—which often serve a business—can create a problem later if a customer switches to another product or opens another account with different terms. The customer thinks that certain services are free, and won't pay unless the value received from the service doubles, according to research performed by leading behavioral economists.[2]

Behavioral economists refer to this as an *anchor price*, and it amounts in practice to consumers believing that a good should cost what they paid the first time they bought it. Charging nothing for a product effectively trains the customer to think that nothing is what it should cost, regardless of value delivered. The effects of anchor pricing have been pervasive throughout the Internet era, when many providers of digital products launched initially free services, or services funded by minimal advertising, with the intention of converting to subscription structures over time. When it came to converting them to pay models, however, the customers were not so willing. Converting online users into paying subscribers has been the challenge of the decade for "build it and they will come" Web companies.

Payer attitudes toward price also work to a seller's disadvantage when the cost to produce a product is far higher than what end customers would pay for it. High-quality newspapers and magazines, for example, are very expensive to produce, with their corps of journalists and editors and printing infrastructure. An economic study conducted in the 1990s estimated that if subscriptions and newsstand prices reflected the full cost of production, the average newspaper would charge an estimated four or five times its newsstand price, assuming circulation stayed constant.[3]

Readers have never seen that real cost, of course. Supplementary revenue from advertisement and classifieds allowed print media moguls to subsidize consumer prices so they could charge $0.50 a day at the newsstand and less for subscriptions. The customer's cost expectation fell in line accordingly. This is true in other industries as well. Ask most people in the United States whether they think gas is too expensive at $2.50 a gallon, and you'll get a resounding "Yes!" The anchor price for most of the population is still around $1.50, the price from fifteen years ago. Such price associations, of course, also spell trouble for renewable energy alternatives, which are being judged subconsciously not just against the cost of gasoline today but against what gasoline "should" cost.

Both of these examples come out of industries where there is a lot of competition from lower-priced alternatives. Both also offer clear evidence that "added value" does not always translate into greater consumer willingness to buy. Conceivably, the perpetuation of a strong and independent press is recognized as a good thing, a baseline requirement for an accountable democratic society. But that does not seem to have helped the U.S. paper of record: the *New York Times* fell on such difficulties from declining readership that it negotiated $250 million in loan capital from Mexican billionaire Carlos Slim in 2009—and it is by no means out of the woods.[4] The company is still trying to figure out a revenue model that works.

The above examples are only illustrative, and certainly not exhaustive, of why sellers with good products sometimes fail to find the right pricing model to capitalize on customer demand. Below we'll explore the pros and cons of the pricing models that have been tried in the media industry and elsewhere in the search for new, workable revenue models. Before that, let me once again call out the importance of using a behavioral segmentation frame as you think about these various models. They may not work for your industry's version of the Massive Passives, but they may open a door to effectively targeting segments with different or emerging behaviors.

Subscriptions

Subscriptions have been a classic pricing model in media for generations, from newspapers and magazines to cable television. Digitization has made it easier to innovate around subscriptions. It also makes possible a shift from traditional subscription models—which are usually limited by either time or consumption volume—to lifetime or unlimited subscriptions. Publishing offers many examples of the ways in which digitization has opened up more subscription flexibility. Instead of limiting newspaper subscription options to "when" you get it (daily, weekend only, or weekday only), digitally delivered content can now be much more tailored along the lines of what you get and how you get it.

German publisher Axel Springer started experimenting with new pricing models for its online general-interest content in December 2009—one of the first in Europe to follow the lead of business newspapers. Springer publishes both the *Bild* tabloid, Europe's widest circulating daily, and the high-quality paper *Die Welt*, which amounts to something like having the *National Enquirer* and the *New York Times* under one corporate umbrella. The first step in Springer's online pay plan involves paid subscriptions through an iPhone app. It is also working with Deutsche Telekom to develop other subscription models—including micropayment options—that would be charged via phone bills.[5]

The *New York Times* is taking a different approach. Since it first went digital, the *Times* has tried, and failed, with a number of subscription approaches, most famously with "*Times* Select," which gave print and online subscribers exclusive access to columnists' articles and the Sunday magazine. The *Times* abandoned its Select service in 2008, choosing to experiment with whether making everything free to readers online could raise traffic and therefore advertising revenue enough to cover costs. It didn't. So, at the end of 2009, the *Times* announced a plan to implement a metered service in 2011 similar to the approach of the *Financial Times*. Metered pricing allows nonsubscribers access to a certain number of articles for free per month, after which they have to pay.[6]

A bolder option for subscription flexibility comes from MagHound, a magazine portal sponsored by Time Inc. MagHound subscribers pay a monthly subscription rate for three, five, or seven titles, just as they would with a direct subscription. But the site allows them to switch out which magazines they receive. So a bride might sign up for *Modern Bride* while she is planning the wedding and switch to *Modern Living* once the wedding has passed. MagHound subscribers still receive the physical magazines, which limits the present flexibility of the service. If the service goes fully digital, however, they can cut and slice the content any way they want—all the recipes from *Food & Wine*, *Every Day with Rachel Ray*, and *Martha Stewart Living*, for instance.

Subscription models are going to get more interesting in the coming years as content providers take advantage not only of the consumer's interest in specific content, but of the propensity to use different devices in different contexts. For instance, the current plan at the *Times* is to continue to let print subscribers access unlimited online content for free. Yet a Kindle subscription is still separate as I write this and not discounted for print readers. Rationality says that consumers won't pay again for something they are already receiving, but history shows that is not true. Media's practice of windowing has long taken advantage of the human tendency to buy the same content in different forms—the DVD of a movie already seen in the theater or on cable, for instance—and even more so with consumers buying their music or movie library again as formats have changed.

Beyond Publishing: Subscription Models in Nontraditional Sectors

Outside of print media, subscriptions can be easily applied to products that consumers use all the time or in a predictable cycle. Regular or cyclical purchases allow the seller to offer what looks like a discount and the buyer to gain in convenience and perceived cost savings. The online music service Napster shifted from music downloads priced by unit, analogous to iTunes' original approach, to offering a streamed music subscription in monthly, quarterly, or annual models. Each subscription includes "credits" for downloading songs so consumers can locally store their favorites. Likewise, Netflix innovated a subscription model in the traditional pay-per-use movie rental sector.

Outside of media, subscriptions have also popped up in sectors that have traditionally relied on other payment models. A number of online stock brokers, for example, offer subscription-like packages of a maximum number of trades for a fixed price per month. New York–based online grocer FreshDirect gives a discounted delivery subscription to its frequent customers—a fixed, prepaid price for six months of "free delivery," compared with a standard $5.95 delivery charge on every order. Amazon's popular Amazon Prime service is a similar annual subscription to a two-day delivery service. Amazon also offers discounts for customers who "subscribe" to certain products by committing to buy high-consumption items (like paper towels, diapers, or dish soap) on a regular basis over a period of time.

AAA's roadside service for flat tires and breakdowns is another example of the successful application of a subscription model in an area where pay-per-use once predominated. Let your subscription lapse, and you may just find you have a flat in a snowstorm. In this instance, customers are happy to pay for a subscription they never use. So goes the psychology of pricing, sometimes.

Similar models have been tried here or there in the U.S. health-care industry—of course, in some ways health insurance is a subscription to health-care services. Given the challenges to the extant business models in the health-care industry, we're seeing more providers start to look at pricing innovations like subscriptions. For instance, Primedic, a primary care service provider in Monterrey, Mexico, offers "membership" to poor community members. Annual fees allow users to access unlimited primary care services at Primedic's three clinics, and discounts on referred services.

Continuity Pricing

Book, music, and collectibles vendors have a variation on subscription pricing called a *continuity* model. In this model, promoted by companies such as BMG, consumers sign up as members and receive a selection every month. If they keep the item, they get billed for it sometime later (books and music are usually discounted, collectibles less so); if they send it back, they pay nothing. These models rely a great deal on consumer inertia, since many people intend to return items but then miss the deadline or decide, product in hand, that the return is just not worth it.

Continuity pricing has been used for music, books, wine-of-the-month clubs, and many other products besides. It seems an approach of the analog age, but with some intelligent behavioral segmentation and sufficiently low pricing, it could be applied to many other products and services, selected by combing customers' preferences with "customers who liked this also liked this" analytics.

Variable Pricing

Readers who access the *New York Times* on their Kindle pay $13.99 a month. Those who get it on their doorstep pay about $25. And the ones who read online pay nothing, minus some of the content. Such altering of price based on platform is an example of *variable pricing*. You can vary the price of the product according to any number of factors, including when the product is purchased, when it is consumed, by whom, on what platform, and in what volume. Pricing can even vary based on old-fashioned popularity. After years of selling songs at $0.99, iTunes has recently introduced variability in its pricing model, with less popular tunes held at $0.99 and top picks bumped up to $1.29. There has been a mild outcry from the public, but that is largely a problem of expectation set by Apple's $0.99 anchor price. Amazon was likewise locked in a bitter battle with publishers in 2010 over instituting variable (and higher) pricing for Kindle-format best sellers. In an effort to increase customers' confidence in and usage of e-books, Amazon tried to set a standard $9.99 price for all e-books, even selling them at that price when it had to pay publishers a higher amount. Publishers, understanding the power of anchor pricing and learning a lesson from the music industry's iTunes experience (which we'll discuss later), have been trying to force Amazon to implement variable pricing. In this instance, that means charging more for new books and best sellers than for the old standbys.

Variable pricing comes in different forms, including simple variation, dynamic pricing, cross-subsidy models such as tiered pricing or "freemiums," or buyer-controlled models such as auction pricing and pay-what-you-want.

Many companies are wary of certain approaches to variable pricing. Existing customers can object to shifts in pricing models, and companies are often concerned about cannibalization within variable pricing models—given a choice, wouldn't all customers end up choosing the cheapest option and hurt revenue and margins? These concerns and challenges are real. Yet the many approaches to variable pricing outlined below show that there is almost always an approach that works for sellers and buyers.

Simple Variable Pricing

As the name suggests, *simple variable pricing* is when prices for an identical good or service vary depending on when or where the product or service is purchased. This includes the ability of different retailers to charge different prices for the same product, or the ability for Central Park water vendors to charge $1.50 for a bottle of water in December and $3.00 for the same bottle in July.

Simple variable pricing is starting to appear in more and more places as it becomes easier to change prices, in terms of both not needing to change a price tag and informing customers of the price. One example is congestion pricing that is starting to appear in many large cities around the world. Congestion pricing for traffic management is a form of simple variable pricing in which cars pay higher tolls to travel during peak traffic times. Congestion pricing has different applications, some absolute and others more limited. For instance, all drivers who travel to inner London during the day are charged a fee for the privilege. New York's Mayor Bloomberg wanted to apply a similar scheme in the Big Apple, but had to settle for simply charging cars $2 more to cross the George Washington Bridge and other access routes into New York City during rush hour.

The dining sector offers another example. As I write this, celebrated Chef Gary Achatz, of the Chicago restaurant Alinea, was planning the Autumn 2010 launch of a new locale that will serve only one fixed menu, which diners reserve as they would a theater ticket, by reserving a seat at one of two time-slots. Ticket prices will vary based on the day of the week—a coveted Saturday ticket will be priced higher than Tuesday, for example.

Dynamic Pricing

The difference between dynamic pricing and simple variable pricing is primarily based on predictability. In simple variable pricing, customers have at least a rough sense of how prices will change from place to place, time to time, or situation to situation. Everyone, for instance, knows that the hotel store at the vacation resort is going to charge far more for souvenirs than the vendors outside. Dynamic pricing is far less predictable—and, of course, far more dynamic. In a *dynamic pricing* model the price of a good or service is determined in the moment by various factors, many of which won't be apparent to the customer. Check the price now and five minutes from now, and it may be different.

Dynamic pricing is the most familiar approach in the travel and hospitality industries, in which the price of an airline ticket or a hotel room dynamically increases or decreases depending on how full the airplane or hotel is and how may days remain until the travel date. Dynamic pricing works in these contexts because the product is literally perishable—its supply is useless after a certain date, just like overripe fruit, which, incidentally, is also priced to move the older it gets.

Dynamic pricing works as well in markets where demand varies by time of day or year. Travel is a traditional arena, but other industries are getting into the act, such as electric utilities or beverages. The Coca-Cola Company has experimented in Japan with vending machines equipped with sensors that increase the price of the product based on outside temperature, or time of day, or remaining supply. The Coke machines up the price to keep at the top of what consumers are willing to pay.[7]

While dynamic pricing has the potential to ensure that a seller gets the highest margin possible, it is also dangerous. Customers can react very negatively if they don't understand the factors that drive pricing changes and don't consider them reasonable. In fact, one form of dynamic pricing is illegal in many places: raising prices dramatically after a natural disaster, commonly called gouging. Getting dynamic pricing right takes a lot of work and research, and a good grounding in pricing theory.[8]

Cross-Subsidies

Cross-subsidies involve giving one product away, or selling it at a deep discount, to generate demand for another. There are three basic types of cross-subsidy: the razor blade model, the reverse razor blade model, and tiered pricing.

The *razor blade* model, named after the first major practitioner, Gillette, which gave away razors in order to sell high-margin razor blades, is applied today to any number of products: Bloomberg terminals used by Wall Street traders, for example, or TiVos. According to peripatetic entrepreneur and consultant Randy Komisar, the founders of TiVo had originally designed their business as a hardware play. After they consulted with Komisar and heard his views on the difficulty of making a profit in devices, they shifted their business plan to take a loss on the hardware and (eventually) earn money on selling proprietary content, such as television listings that the unique TiVo interface and software can take advantage of.[9] Cable companies do no different when they rent set-top boxes or cable modems for a few dollars a month, while making money on the services delivered through those devices. And cellular service companies rely on a similar strategy when they subsidize or give away the phone and make up the difference in subscription plans and add-ons.

The second, and increasingly popular, alternative in cross-subsidies is the *reverse razor blade* approach offered by companies such as Apple or Amazon. Apple sells its own devices at top dollar, and then has a store for the sale of integrated content and applications that work on Apple devices. The content adds value to the device and helps lock in customers, and Apple makes money by taking a cut of App Store sales. The real money for Apple, however, comes from the razor—the iPhone, iPod, and iPad that consumers buy and replace in two- to three-year cycles. For Apple, songs and apps are the inexpensive blades that give the profitable razor its value. The same goes for Amazon with its Kindle reader (razor) and e-books (blade). In many cases Amazon is charging less than it pays for Kindle-version books.

A third form of cross-subsidy is *tiered pricing*, in which one set of customers effectively subsidizes another by paying a higher price for the product. For example, pharmaceutical companies have made drugs available at low cost to people living in developing countries, partly by charging market price in wealthier economies. In the digital space, subsidizers are rewarded with more product or additional functionality.

Freemiums are commonly offered within a tiered pricing structure. Coined by venture capitalist Fred Wilson, *freemiums* are free, stripped-down versions of products, built to allow a customer to test the product, risk free. There is some content available free to readers online, while a paid subscription lets readers see more. The *Wall Street Journal* is constantly adjusting and adding tiers as it tries to find an optimum revenue model.

Freemiums are most popular in software. Intuit, like most vendors of consumer tax software, offers a free version of its popular tax preparation software, TurboTax, for filers who have only the most basic tax returns. The free versions are useful, but for anything beyond the 1040EZ form—capital gains, a home office deduction, say, or a new income source—you need one of the more functional versions, which start around $29.95 and go up from there in price and complexity. Intuit also used to offer a free, online version of Quicken, its home accounting tool. It was beaten in the free, online space by Mint, a start-up that made money via advertising and sponsorship—a reminder that every company needs to be thinking about all the different types of revenue innovation simultaneously. Ultimately, Intuit threw in the towel on its free version of Quicken and acquired Mint to be the "free" part of its freemium model.

The Internet, of course, is rich with freemiums, like Skype's free VOIP calling service for calls to other Skype users, and Map-MyRun.com, which offers a free mapping tool so hobby runners can see how many miles their favorite routes cover. For a few extra dollars a month, MapMyRun users can use the workout tracker and get professional advice on ways to adjust workouts to meet fitness or weight-loss goals. Parent company MapMyFit-ness also has associated iPhone apps.

User-Controlled: Auction Pricing, Pay-What-You-Want, and Pay-for-Performance

Variable pricing very overtly asks sellers to think about their audience in segments based on consumption (both volume and complexity), venue, and willingness to pay. This is less obvious than it seems. Most companies think of reward-based discount-ing when they innovate around their most loyal or high-volume consumers. But variable pricing models—especially tiered pric-ing—suggest that the customer who uses the service the most is the one who finds the most value and therefore is most willing to pay more.

Auction models, pay-what-you-want, and *pay-for-performance* very overtly take into account the idea that different consumers may be willing to pay different prices for the same product. Instead of advertising multiple prices, these models let the customer decide. EBay is obviously the undisputed master of consumer online auctions, but there are plenty of cotravelers. Priceline, for example, applies something of an auction model to rental cars and hotel rooms and airline tickets. The customer states what they are willing to pay, and Priceline looks for a match. Reverse auctions (where suppliers compete based on who has the lowest bid) became popular through sites like E-Loan and LendingTree. Some of the corporate supplier portals that emerged in the late 1990s also employed auction or reverse auction models, with the demand side stating what they would pay and the supply side stating what they would take.

Auction pricing is now becoming common in advertising, as online platforms such as Google's AdSense automate the sale of ad space. The top slots go to the highest bidders, but the price also adjusts based on the number of bids and the volume of availability.

The niche approach of pay-what-you-want deserves special mention as well. The rock band Radiohead gained attention in 2007 when it released its album *In Rainbows* on its Web site and gave fans the ability to choose their own price. The band followed with a box set version a few months later, which reportedly sold one hundred thousand copies at a price point of $81—but that was only after *In Rainbows* had been downloaded more than a million times, with 40 percent of downloaders paying an average $6 for the album.[10]

Current efforts to overhaul the U.S. health-care system have led pharmaceutical firms and insurance companies to entertain pay-for-performance models around certain drugs. The idea came out of a deal that Johnson & Johnson (J&J) established with the British National Health Service (NHS) in 2007 around the drug Velcade. Although the drug had been approved to treat a specific type of cancer, the NHS had determined that it was not cost effective, and would not approve it for use in Britain. J&J kept a foothold in the U.K. market by agreeing to charge NHS only for patients for whom the drug was effective, as measured by tumor shrinkage of more than 50 percent.

Since J&J's early experiment, pay-for-performance models have shown up in experiments by Novartis and Merck. From a revenue perspective, pay-for-performance at first glance may be a mixed bag, since a number of popular drugs prescribed to treat common ailments are ineffective for some patients with the disease. Antidepressants do not work for 38 percent of the people for whom they are prescribed, popular arthritis medication is ineffective for 50 percent of sufferers, and cancer medications cannot help up to 75 percent of those with the disease.[11] Pharmaceutical companies clearly want to sell as much medication as they can to earn back their research investment. This is not to say they don't care whether their drugs are effective—a highly effective drug is always going to be more financially successful than a wishy-washy one. But the decentralized, multiparty setup of the health-care system means that pharmaceutical companies historically have had little incentive, once a drug was approved, to conduct more trials to identify the profile of the optimal patient, and little ability to capture and analyze useful data on a drug's effectiveness in the real world. Absent other options, pharmaceutical firms are left with selling some drugs to everyone, rather than a lot of drugs to the right people.

Pay-for-performance offers one promising way to correct the mixed incentives in pharmaceutical delivery. It is only really possible because of the advancements in information technology and the expansion of electronic patient records that are beginning to allow all parts of the system to collect better information about who is on what drug combinations and how they are faring. And let's not forget the patient. Drugs often do not work alone, and they don't always work if they aren't taken properly. Some pay-for-performance experiments involve patient compliance in the mix. CIGNA and Merck, for instance, have hit on a discounting and cost-sharing model that includes data about patient compliance in the drug regimen for type 2 diabetes control.[12] In other words, behavioral segmentation is opening the door for much more successful pricing innovation in the pharmaceutical industry.

By Parts

Companies in sectors as varied as apparel and financial services have tended to limit the forms in which their products are offered so they can serve the greatest number of clients with the least amount of variation. For physical goods and high-touch service industries, the cost to create, deliver, and manage different cuts of the same product was too high, compared with the revenues.

In the digital world, physical limitations are mostly gone for information products. It usually costs a company very little to reconfigure a digital product and very little to deliver it (ignoring, of course, variations in standards or network costs). So products that could only come in one analog form can now be cut up into components that are priced and sold according to their perceived value.

Componentization is part of the chapter on packaging. The difference between *componentization* as a packaging strategy and *by parts* as a pricing strategy has to do largely with how the product is put to use. Componentization in its most interesting iterations puts the component to a different use from the whole part. So a ringtone is used to signal that a call is coming in, while the whole song is used as a form of entertainment. The ringtone is therefore a component; the song is a part.

For a long time the music industry resisted, and then relented on, selling music by parts instead of as whole albums. The publisher of this book, Harvard Business Review Press, sells chapters of classic titles for $6.95 a piece, a particularly attractive model for managers with little time, or students who need to read only part of a book for class.

Selling parts instead of the whole can be revenue-positive in many industries, such as electronics or automotive, where the part may be needed to operate the whole and so can be priced at a premium. Selling by parts is not necessarily a revenue-positive move in media, however. Few fourteen-song albums contain fourteen songs that people want to listen to. More often there are just two or three songs. By allowing customers to buy just the three songs, music companies took a big revenue hit.

But that's not the whole story. While short-term revenues decline, there could also be big wins in customer satisfaction and loyalty. The music industry continues to ignore the fact that its revenue model collapsed because customers hated it. Years of being forced to buy fourteen songs you didn't want to get two you did bred a lot of ill will. Too many companies in other industries are repeating this same mistake. Sticking it to the customer may be profitable, but only as long as the customer lacks options. Sacrificing fat margins by experimenting with new pricing models may be the wiser course for firms and industries that don't want to see the 40 percent drops in revenue experienced by the big music labels.

Bundling Versus À La Carte

A variation on by-parts pricing is the *à la carte* model, which gives customers the option to choose their individual preferences from a menu of items. À la carte options almost by definition coexist in markets where a *bundled* alternative is available, just as in some restaurants diners can select the prix fixe option or make their own—usually more expensive—selections from the menu.

Bundles show up everywhere. In the automotive industry, the Japanese manufacturers introduced the practice in the 1970s of bundling features such as automatic locks and windows, sunroofs, and air-conditioning and selling them at a "discount"; now it's hard to buy a car any other way. The travel industry also sells packages or bundles. These vary from the simple bundling of airline travel and hotel reservations for one destination, to complex, multisite itineraries including tour guides and restaurants and site visits.

Bundles in these contexts are seen as a customer service—an advantage that makes the purchase less complicated or cheaper.

In contrast, à la carte models can cater to a customer's desire for choice and flexibility. Neither, of course, is a guaranteed win. A poorly executed à la carte model can make the customer feel taken advantage of, as with air travelers who are now required to pay separately for baggage handling or drinks service or meals on formerly full-service—and still full-price—airlines. Forced bundling can do the same, as we are starting to see in cable.

Bundled subscriptions have been the only revenue model available in cable television. A small à la carte element comes into play in the fact that the carriers let customers buy add-ons like HBO at a premium. This mixed approach evolved as an imperfect solution to the real difficulty of knowing what the average consumer would pay for most channels. By bundling content, the cable company could deliver the same product to everyone, and the customer could self-customize simply by watching what he wanted; the more popular content thus cross-subsidized the less popular.

Time has only made the cable pricing ecosystem more complex. Specialty channels like HBO are now increasingly available in bundles. Optional add-ons like high-definition, all-sports packages, cable broadband, and telephone service have saddled customers with a bewildering set of options and fees. The net effect has been to produce confusion for content providers, cable companies, and customers, and to stymie any attempt to gain useful information about the customer's willingness to pay.

That wouldn't be such a problem but for the increasing influence of default à la carte offerings from YouTube, Hulu, iTunes, and their digital peers. An increasing number of Gadgetiers and Massive Passives are now wondering why they are paying their cable providers for two hundred channels but watching only fifteen.[13] Why not pay for the fifteen they watch, and ditch the rest? Even more exaggerated behaviors come from the Kool Kids, who are coming of age with on-demand access to anytime, anywhere content.

Fortunately, cable providers now have the technology to unbundle the channels and deliver just what the customer wants at no additional delivery cost. The set-top box also collects viewing information, so theoretically the providers could make the à la carte selection process very easy for the customer by preidentifying "favorites" that a customer could opt out of.

Of course, the content providers are often one of the biggest roadblocks to innovation from the cable companies, because such pricing innovations have the potential to disrupt their business models. À la carte pricing, for instance, strikes at the heart of the deal that the content providers have negotiated with cable companies: they charge a bit less than they could for the most popular channels while charging more for the more obscure channels. This deal helps the content providers maximize distribution of their niche channels; the slow breakdown of this deal is causing internal tension at the content providers as the heads of the more popular channels see that they would benefit from an à la carte model where they could raise prices, while the heads of less popular channels are deathly afraid of à la carte pricing.

Outside of the United States a number of cable providers are experimenting with these possibilities. Hanaro Telecom of Korea offers a pay-per-view model through its HanaroTV platform; in its first year of operation, it gained five hundred thousand customers. Canal+ in France offers half-price weekend-only sub-scriptions, while PCCW's Now TV in Hong Kong lets its eight hundred thousand subscribers customize their packages to include only the channels they want.[14]

Despite these existing examples, many executives in cable are resisting the call to à la carte out of fear of lost revenue. Those same executives want to shift the digitally savvy customer to what Comcast, for instance, is calling TV Everywhere—a kind of passport service that provides subscribers with a log-in they can use to access content via any device they want: television, computer, pay-per-view via streamed video. There is certainly room in the market for such an approach, but it can't be the only option. TV Everywhere and its brethren look a lot like what the music labels did with albums—they want to continue selling everything to everyone. We know where that leads. The longer the cable industry clings to a bundle-only pricing model, the wider the door swings open for nontraditional competition: single-show downloads from iTunes, or the newer à la carte streaming services available from iTunes, Amazon, and Net-flix. There's also on-demand content available from start-up providers like Sezmi, which downloads content from traditional television, cable, or Internet onto a TV-attached hard drive. And don't forget the customization and alternatives that Google TV could ultimately deliver.

Why let things get contentious? À la carte selection of digital content creates the potential for the positive creation of more flexible products suited to either *what* the customer watches or *when* they watch. It is not difficult to imagine a near future in which a sports-loving customer chooses among a few options: a transactional à la carte pay-per-view model that allows him to pay only for what he watches, a "sports" product that bundles the main sports channels, or an all-inclusive weekend-only package priced at half the cost of a full-time unlimited delivery.

I by no means underestimate the challenge. The cable operators earn more than 95 percent of revenue directly from the consumer.[15] Unbundling puts a portion of that revenue at risk, as it may wake customers up to what they were absentmindedly watching simply because it was "part of the package." Regardless, a shift toward à la carte is truly inevitable. Hulu, iTunes, Netflix, and now Amazon already offer default à la carte programming: Hulu in an ad-supported model with a subscription add-on for its more popular content, and iTunes in pay-per-download, with both streaming and rent-per-download models likely in the works. Game consoles like Wii and Xbox likewise have on-demand video functions. If the cable industry does not take a dominant role in setting the terms and price of à la carte viewing, then these competitors will, and the story may follow the path of digital music. And for all industry observers out there who think this is only a challenge for cable, remember that bundling is a part of the pricing models of many other industries, from automotive to travel to software suites.

But Maybe À La Carte Isn't So Bad . . .

In a delightfully ironic twist, there are people within the cable industry who are championing unbundling—namely, in broadband. Cable network service providers like Time Warner Cable and Comcast are trying to figure out how to shift broadband service from the standard unlimited subscription model. The reason is bandwidth.

Data transfers from e-mail or static Web sites do not require much bandwidth. Thus, when Internet service providers (ISPs) were trying to push customers to pricier broadband plans and away from dial-up or DSL, they offered unlimited subscriptions that made their services seem cheap, and encouraged "surfers" to linger on the portals that ISPs like AOL and Microsoft (MSN) had built. But the explosion of high-bandwidth applications like high-quality video is quickly crashing the old model.

This shift in traffic volumes has not taken the industry entirely by surprise. Pundits have been pointing for decades to a switch to video and voice over computer networks (even well before the Internet existed). Most people inside and outside the industry never believed the transition would happen as fast as it is (a cautionary tale for other industries about how fast technology can shatter your business model if ever there was one).

The doubters were wrong. Data traffic over the Internet and mobile devices is projected to grow 6,400 percent between 2008 and 2013, mostly on the back of video streaming, which is expected to make up 56 percent of network traffic.[16] Cable providers can see the explosion in traffic. Likewise, they can see that their revenues are staying flat, despite booms in volume, because their unlimited pricing model prevents them from monetizing increased usage. Many of the broadband providers are dipping their toes in the water by charging more for faster speeds. The first move to truly get away from unlimited usage has come from AT&T in the wireless space, which stopped offering unlimited data plans to new customers in June 2010. Other broadband providers will continue to watch AT&T's experiment, and others will join them before long, no doubt.

Rent Versus Buy

Another pricing option is to let consumers rent a product previously available through sell-through. The rental option is particularly interesting in tough economic times, as movie rental vending machine provider Redbox is seeing in the rental film industry, or in luxury industries, as Rent the Runway is seeing in fashion.

I mentioned Redbox in the chapter on segmentation, where I called the company out as another new competitor in the movie rental business. Although it is operating in an already-mature market, Redbox is innovating the film rental industry by decreasing the brick-and-mortar footprint, cannibalizing traffic from other popular retailers, and pushing the price low enough that the customers are thinking differently about renting versus buying. Redbox has done this by placing movie rental vending machines in high-traffic locations such as grocery stores, and pricing the rental at $1.00 a night, compared with the $4.99 multinight rental from Blockbuster and other brick-and-mortar players. In short, Redbox is making renting so convenient and the pricing so low that it changes the economic calculation in the mind of the viewer.

It used to be that if a moviegoer liked a movie, he would go out and buy the DVD when it was released. Most buyers could easily imagine watching a well-liked movie three times or more, and with the rental price from Blockbuster at $4.99 a night, one could buy the DVD and own it for about the same amount spent on rentals. Redbox blows up this calculation. While it is easy to imagine watching the same movie three or four times, it is very difficult to imagine watching it the fifteen or twenty times needed to get to the same price point. Redbox's selection is limited to recent and popular movies, but customers don't seem to mind. Rental revenue was up by 8 percent in the first half of 2009, with vending machine rentals capturing 19 percent of the movie rental market share, mostly at the expense of brick-and-mortar revenues.[17] In contrast, DVD sales were down by 13.5 percent in the first half of 2009.[18]

For those who still want to buy the video, Redbox indirectly has a solution for them too: secondhand sales. Half of Redbox's DVDs get resold on the used market at a price point far below the $20 retail price that studios are used to getting for new releases. So while studios like Fox, Universal, and Disney aren't crazy about the low rental price point, they are just as concerned about the impact Redbox has on the sell-through DVD market from dumping used DVD inventory onto secondhand dealers. The response of a few of the studios, including Fox, Universal, and Warner, has been to limit Redbox's access to new content for a period of about four weeks after a new release (Netflix is also subject to these access limitations). Redbox was working around some of these limits by buying the releases at retail value from Walmart.[19] Under extreme pressure from the studios, both Netflix and Redbox have recently struck agreements to not carry new releases for four weeks after DVDs go on sale.[20]

Despite the consternation of the studios, Redbox, and the low-cost kiosk rental model in general, seems unstoppable.

Blockbuster is playing catch-up by launching kiosks of its own, and by December 2009, there were more than fifty thousand DVD vending machines stocked with around two hundred titles. The vending industry will get even more interesting when digital pricing and signage is far enough along to allow any consumer with a hankering and a USB stick to sidle up to a machine and download a film—several companies with this model will launch in 2010.

A New Twist on Auto Rental

Another company adding a different twist on a mature rental industry is Zipcar, the car-sharing service available in many U.S. cities. Unlike traditional rental companies such as Avis or Hertz, Zipcar allows its members to reserve cars on the phone or over the Internet for as little as an hour. The cars sit between reservations in preassigned parking lots, and are set up with automatic smart locks that open when members swipe an ID card. All cars have either keyless ignitions or keys attached inside the car, so there is no chance that the driver will lose keys and no key drop-off or pickup to worry about. Gas, mileage, and accident insurance are all included in the hourly charge, and Zipcar has identification and payment information on record for each associated Zipster, so there is no need to "check in" or "check out." Zipcar's pricing structure includes a monthly subscription for high-volume drivers, or a simple per-use model (with higher hourly rates) that charges only when a driver actually uses a car.

Zipcar's self-declared raison d'être is to take cars off the road by offering urbanites a convenient alternative to ownership, but it seems to save a lot of money too: the average American household spends 18 percent of income on transportation; the average car-sharing member only 6 percent. Even accounting for differences between urban and suburban energy consumption, that's a lot of money.[21] Those hourly rentals are expected to earn Zipcar $130 million in 2009.[22] This pricing innovation and general business model has now been extended to bikes in urban areas from Berlin to Mexico City, with generally positive results.

Rental Models in Sell-Through Industries

Video and car rental are both mature markets, but rental is taking hold as well in unexpected sectors. As I mentioned at the beginning of this chapter, fashion is exploring rental options through new ventures like Rent the Runway and a similar company that provides handbags, From Bags to Riches.

Rental structures in the sell-through world of retail fashion are not without precedent. Department stores have rented dresses, suits, and jewelry for years, particularly for high-end products worn by wealthy or well-known clients. Then there is default rental where the customer buys the dress with the intention of wearing it once before bringing it back. But Rent the Runway and From Bags to Riches have expanded the geographic potential of legitimate fashion rental services, making it possible for a debutante in Ohio to get the same Carolina Herrera dress she saw Paris Hilton wear in *People* for less than she might have paid for something off the rack from her local Macy's. And this is not just for dresses. From Bags to Riches, a St. Paul, Minnesota–based concern launched in 2004, offers original brand-name bags for rent from between $22.95 and $299.00 a month.

Seasonal businesses in sell-through industries also show potential for rental alternatives. During the 2008 holiday season, a landscaper who'd seen demand for his services drop in the down economy piloted a Christmas tree rental service in Los Angeles. He provides live trees to renters, who decorate and keep them for three weeks, after which he picks them up, alive, and stores them for the year at various outdoor sites in the city. The rental price is comparable to a tree purchase, minus the hassle of pickup and disposal and the piles of dry needles on the living room carpet. Customers also get the "green glow" from an apparently more environmentally friendly product. That green motivation is, by the way, one of the major drivers of rental models—and a ripe target market with the proper combination of VALS and behavioral segmentation.

Pricing Innovation Pitfalls

Historically, pricing experiments were not very risky. Customers in one segment or region could not easily see what was offered elsewhere. But digitization has made it quite easy for consumers to compare products based on features, availability, and price, and not just at home in front of the computer. Mobile apps such as ShopSavvy allow mobile phone users to take a picture of a bar code in the store and do an Internet search for the best price. That means you have legitimate reason to be concerned about a pricing experiment becoming a "hit" when you don't want it to.

While digitization makes pricing experiments more risky in some ways, it also makes them easier. Digitization and online selling and inventory management have removed some of the infrastructure barriers to frequent price changes. No longer do employees have to physically walk around the store retagging everything. Changes instead can be made within a central system and reflected across the store or on the Internet. Informing a target segment of a new pricing structure is also vastly less costly than it used to be.

The increased technical ease with which comparisons and price changes can occur has not caused much change in company practices, however. There has been real, historical hesitancy by incumbent players to experiment with pricing models. Most of this hesitancy is caused by inertia and risk avoidance, but there remains a well-founded perception that pricing changes result in lost revenues, angry customers, and management difficulties. Brokerage firm Charles Schwab—famous for the way it capitalized on the digital economy—experienced some of those challenges in the late-1990s explosion of Internet trading.

The problems came about when Charles Schwab launched an online option called e.Schwab aimed at capturing the customer segment that wanted to trade via the Internet—a group served by discount brokers E*Trade, Datek, and others with supercheap pricing models for frequent traders. E.Schwab customers paid a low monthly subscription and received a certain number of trades—but little personal service. Calls to telephone service agents were limited to one per month, and walk-in consultations in Schwab branches were fully reserved for full-service customers still paying trade commissions.[23]

The result of this experiment was that e.Schwab customers were annoyed that they couldn't get help whenever they needed it, and the full-service customers were annoyed that they still had to pay trade commissions. There was also some internal fighting at Schwab because of the administrative challenge of managing two customer relationship models with no crossover (customers with existing full-service accounts could not at that time integrate their e.Schwab account with their full-service product).

Schwab eventually determined that two-tiered pricing would not work for the company, and it merged the e.Schwab and full-service models into one approach that offered less expensive, more service-oriented online and brick-and-mortar trading for everyone. Trade commissions went away, and the average transaction earnings dropped, but the company eventually made up the difference in new accounts, and it did become for a time the largest online broker, handling more than 20 percent of online trades.[24]

Remove the specifics of Schwab, and the relevant dynamics apply to any number of industries: there is pressure from both the upper and the lower end of the market; there are customer expectations of a certain level of service at any price; there are customers wanting greater control over their choices; and there is overall fear of change.

Companies that have not yet experimented with pricing innovation may look at the challenges and reject pricing innovation in an effort to protect what they have. The examples used in this chapter partly bear that out. Redbox, Zipcar, HannaroTV, and Rent the Runway are all new entrants whose pricing models are in the process of changing the economics of their respective markets. In contrast, incumbent cable channels, newspapers, record labels, video rental companies, or software vendors have dragged their feet out of fear that new pricing options will erode revenues from the existing pricing model faster than new customers can be acquired.

The pricing strategies outlined in this chapter may seem familiar, but when applied in nontraditional ways, all come with significant challenges. Some of those challenges are straightforward. Unbundling, for example, coincided with the 40 percent music label revenue loss discussed earlier. Some of the revenue has gone to piracy. Some of it has shifted to different parts of the value chain—live shows, for example, instead of recordings. And some of it has been lost because à la carte pricing allows listeners to spend $2 on the songs they want rather than $14 on the entire album. It would be naive and misleading to claim that unbundling in other industries—such as cable, software, or automotive—will never result in similar revenue-negative results. It may for *some* players serving *some* segments, but I do not believe that has to be the story for all. In fact, it is possible that value will shift to different parts of the value chain. Just as Apple captured music industry value for the device through its lowball pricing of the music, we may see players like TiVo, Google TV, or Sezmi helping shift the value role away from the content providers and toward the devices that make that content accessible and searchable. In other words, the revenue impact from doing nothing may be much worse than the revenue impact of unbundling.

Straightforward loss of revenue is pretty clear-cut. Other challenges to pricing innovation involve subtleties of human psychology. Variable pricing, for example, has a problematic history largely because customers in certain contexts do not like to feel that they are paying more than someone else for the same product, regardless of what they independently might have said that product was worth. Airline passengers intuitively understand that the price of their seat changes depending on the route, time of week or day, position in the cabin, and how far in advance they purchase the ticket, along with other factors. But it still stinks to find out at 30,000 feet that you are enjoying the discomforts of coach for a price twice what your neighbor paid. Variable pricing, particularly dynamic pricing, can leave some customers feeling screwed.

Airlines and other companies in the hospitality industry are working to soften customer ire by making those differences more transparent and ensuring that those who pay more also receive something more—express check-in or waived baggage charges or a guaranteed seat assignment. Suffice it to say that sensitivity to customer perception is a real concern.

Then there are the challenges of finding the right balance of what to charge who via what channels. These balance issues are most evident with subscriptions. Look to any of the major print publications, and you will see a company struggling to find a way to charge for content that readers have come to view as free. In contrast to the *New York Times* and the *Washington Post*, the *Wall Street Journal*, the *Financial Times*, and the *Economist* have all had some form of pay content model since the inception of the Internet. All three are holding their own, and yet the nearly constant changes around what is free and what is not on what platforms at what time show that they have yet to hit on the ideal balance.

The difficulty of finding a working model is exacerbated by ongoing asymmetry of need between seller and buyer. Unlimited consumption subscriptions offer a useful example: for the provider to make money online, the majority of users need to consume less than they are paying for. But the user still needs to perceive sufficient value (which may come in the form of convenience or ease of access). That's a tough circle to square, as the broadband providers are learning. When you are looking at subscription models in general, and unlimited consumption models in particular, the key question to ponder is how well you can forecast consumer behavior and use. Of course, subscription models work best when the marginal costs of delivering more of the product or service approach zero.

Last, it should be noted that not all companies are entirely in control of the factors that drive their pricing model. This is particularly a factor in industries where there is significant revenue sharing, such as in the feature film industry. The studios that distribute feature films take a percentage of theater ticket sales (typically the percentage declines each week after release) but also require a minimum total payment per screen. Those minimum amounts are set high enough that the theater has little incentive to offer discounted tickets or otherwise innovate around price—it needs to make its money back on the tickets without dipping into concession revenues. You see, theaters make most of their profits off concessions (which they don't have to share with the studios), and there is general wisdom that viewers budget for movie dates with an anchor price that varies depending on the city. For New York or Los Angeles, a movie seen in the theater might fetch an anchor of around

$16–$18 per person. If the ticket price is $8, the viewer will spend $8 on food and drink; if the ticket is $12, she will spend only $4 at the concession. Theaters would love to lower the price of tickets to make more on concessions. That's why studios set a minimum rights fee. Neither is particularly movable on the subject, which makes pricing innovation difficult in industries that have a divide between product creation and distribution.

Lessons in Pricing Innovation

Despite the challenges incumbents will face when innovating around their pricing models, new pricing applied in established industries is an inevitable reality of digitization. Incumbent players may be fighting to maintain the revenues they have today, but they cannot be blind to the changes taking place in their own industries. The long-distance telecommunications market has experienced 80 percent declines in revenue over the past eight years, as people migrate to VOIP applications like Skype and Google Talk rather than reach out and touch someone. Music labels have already lost the right to determine the price of a single song, and are fighting to make up the difference by taking a share of value from other parts of the industry.

Pricing innovators also need to be open to experimenting with different pricing models for different customer segments. A segment-oriented play is particularly critical because pricing innovation may indeed lead to revenue cannibalization for some segments while opening opportunities for others. For example, we are seeing right now that Redbox rentals are likely cannibalizing DVD purchases, eating away at revenue faster. So how can the film distributors win some of that revenue back? One alternative is to target a behavioral segment that consumes a great deal of filmed entertainment with a passport movie service that captures more revenue by allowing customers, at a fixed price, to watch the movie in the theater, stream the content onto their devices, and get the physical DVD. Passport customers may also be willing to sign up for a continuity model that gives them "movie everywhere" access to, say, thirty films a year.

Pricing innovation allows for a lot of creative experimentation, but innovators should also take a page from Schwab's book and be willing to change directions if something is not working. Schwab was the first major brokerage firm to come to market with an Internet trading option, and it tried to create a tiered option for the different segments of its customer base. It was a smart attempt, and tiered pricing is a successful play for many companies, but it wasn't for Schwab. The company had built its culture in the 1970s by offering a less expensive, less hand-holding brokerage alternative to Merrill Lynch and Morgan Stanley. So a "full-service" Schwab was not full-service enough to handily separate it from e.Schwab—and everyone, no matter how independent, likes to get a human being on the phone when they need one.

The second lesson from Schwab and others is that different pricing models need to be structured so that it is clear to the customer what they are getting (or not getting). It used to be so difficult to compare prices and models that companies could keep their pricing experiments a relative secret. That opacity is gone now, which makes it hard to experiment discreetly. Perhaps the best option, then, is to embrace transparency, which requires you to really think through what the different structures are and how to make clear to customers the relationship between what they pay for and what they receive. Likewise, customer service agents have to be trained to explain the difference in product categories in such a way that the customer understands what they get for the extra money they pay.

The last lesson is to collaborate with other players within the value chain. When multiple participants share in the revenue stream, they need to work together or collectively watch the opportunity pass. Working at cross-purposes, or simply not cooperating, often generates new offerings that are simply too confusing or too hard for customers to evaluate. When that happens, they tend to just ignore the new product. There may even be opportunities to work with competitors in joint ventures. For industries undergoing rapid revenue erosion, another form of radical pricing transparency may be necessary both to help customers learn the true cost of what they consume and also, without collusion, to drive the evolution of pricing schemes in the entire industry. Rupert Murdoch and the *New York Times* seem to be doing this by speculating about future pricing models in public and/or making announcements about planned changes well before they are implemented.

Getting Started

Table 2-1 provides a brief summary of pricing innovation. What are some of the questions you should ask around strategy,

TABLE 2-1

Pricing innovation in brief

Model	Traditional mode	Innovation	Digital-era example
Subscriptions	Defined by time limit and one-size-fits-all content	Flexibility around what the subscriber receives, when, and in what volume. Subscriptions also applied in new industries	• MagHound • Netflix • Primedic • Amazon Prime
Variable pricing	Altering what a customer pays based on demand for a product or its "perishability"	Cross-subsidy models; freemiums, razor blade or reverse razor blade models; auction models	• Coca-Cola vending • Apple apps • Turbo Tax • Google AdSense
By parts	Products sold in only one format	Products broken into parts sold for the same purpose	• Individual songs • Book chapters (HBP)
Bundling vs. à la carte	Bundled pricing to maximize revenue and cross-subsidize less popular products	À la carte options priced for customers who derive maximum value	• Cable TV industry • Canal + • Broadband access • Automotive options • Travel
Rentals	Rental models applied in traditional rental markets, such as automotive and video, with inflexible time frames and pricing models	Rental models in sell-through markets, or with flexibility around price and time	• Rent the Runway • Zipcar • Redbox

infrastructure, and operations when considering how to pursue pricing innovation?

Strategy

- How does the perception of your product, company, and brand value vary across your customer segments?

- What behavioral segments point to different value perceptions?

- Are some of your consumers more active than others?

- Is some of your functionality used more by some segments than others?

- Do consumers have established price and service-level associations with your company or brand that may be difficult to overcome?

- Do you share the revenue from sales of your product with other participants in the value chain?

Infrastructure

- Do you have the infrastructure to enable new forms of pricing, including micropayments, subscriptions, and universal access?

- Do you have the ability to capture segment-driven pricing results and use it to drive further refinement?

Operations

- What are the implications of pricing changes on your partner ecosystem?

- Can you change prices quickly and seamlessly?

- Are employees able and willing to "sell" the rationale for price variation and generate customer support?

3

Payer Innovation

n the summer of 2007, teens and college students in the United Kingdom got an offer they couldn't refuse: completely free cellular service. Promoted as a hip and exclusive option in nightclubs, cafés, and young-adult hot spots, a new mobile phone company headquartered in Finland called Blyk was doing something unheard of in the mobile telecommunications space: it was giving all its minutes away. Users just needed to order a free SIM card from the company and register on the Web site to talk and receive texts, no charge. There was a catch, though: six times a day, Blyk users were required to listen to an advertising spot. At a time when mobile penetration had reached saturation and mobile advertising represented less than 1 percent of total U.K. ad revenues, Blyk launched an ad-supported telecommunications model that threw away the standard revenue models in mobile.[1] Blyk's goal for its first twelve months was to acquire one hundred thousand users, but it had that many in six months and reached a user base of two hundred thousand by April 2009.[2]

Payer Innovation:
Let's Have a (Third) Party

Blyk's use of advertising in an industry that usually relies on direct revenues is an example of *payer innovation*. Since nothing's free, someone always pays. Payer innovation involves altering *who*. Various payer models already have a long and familiar history in media, and their lessons can be easily extracted and applied to other industries from the current struggles in print and television.

Payer innovation involves the creation of revenue sources that separate the end customer from the person who actually pays, so that there are at least three parties to every transaction instead of two. Advertising sales is the classic example, its value mostly calculated by the number of "impressions" or viewers captured. Other third-party revenue sources include fee-based product placement and sponsorship, advertising's first cousins. This chapter presents examples and possibilities of all three. There are also separate sections on white labeling and social networks and communities, since Facebook and its peers have the potential to monetize an existing intangible asset common to many firms: information about customer preferences and behaviors. Their success or failure offers interesting lessons for sellers, advertisers, and sponsors alike. See figure 3-1 for an overview of payer innovation models.

FIGURE 3-1

Payer innovation models

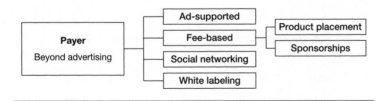

For simplicity's sake, I'll use *indirect revenue* as a catch-all phrase for payer models that involve more than just the consumer of value. Indirect revenue can mean other things in other contexts—here it simply means a payer model where revenue does not flow directly from the consumer of value to the producer of value.

Some readers may be wondering what advertising and sponsorship have to do with innovation. Certainly, indirect revenue models have enjoyed a long and prosperous history. Given the turmoil in advertising markets over the last several years, it also may not seem like a promising way to escape from revenue fluctuations in existing business models.

But there are opportunities for innovation and building new revenue streams in three ways. First, when indirect revenue models are applied to industries or products that historically relied on direct revenue, as Blyk did for telecom. Second, when a traditional, one-to-many advertiser takes advantage of digital platforms to target and interact with consumers in a segmented or individualized way—these advertisers are in effect going "beyond advertising." The third opportunity comes in applying indirect revenue models to products and services where information of considerable value to multiple parties can be gathered and shared, such as social networks (see figure 3-1).

When Direct Revenue Models Fail

Direct revenue models assume that the payer and the user of the product are one and the same. Direct revenue is not the same as wholesale—there can be any number of resellers or intermediaries between the end user and the actual maker of a good and still be a direct revenue source, so long as the value chain is continuous between the maker and the user.

The music industry, for example, has long earned direct revenues from retail sales of vinyl records, cassettes, and CDs, and now MP3s; individual artists and booking agents gain more direct revenue from their cut of concert ticket sales, and music publishers gain by selling usage rights on copyrighted material. This book was sold through a direct revenue model (though digital books could change that structure). Most any physical item one can buy—electronics, appliances, apparel, and most consumables—is sold within a direct revenue model. Direct revenues have historically worked terrifically in a world where sellers make tangible things for which users are willing and able to pay.

For a long time, mobile telecommunications was one of those markets. Mobile providers modeled their revenue structure by allowing subscribers to pay a monthly rate in exchange for airtime and texts, and, more recently, data; others could buy SIM cards pre-loaded with a certain number of minutes. These direct approaches work great for professionals who have the steady income to pay for subscriptions; they even work for people whose income is not so steady, or whose credit history will not allow them to get a subscription contract, but whose phone use is low or variable. It is less of a hit for those with limited disposable money, a fair amount of free time, and a high propensity to talk.

As mentioned, young, technology-savvy consumers are attractive to advertisers because their tastes and loyalties are still fluid, and capturing them is seen as a cost-effective way to attract interest and generate brand recognition now, and profit from them later. Given their willingness to try new products, young consumers also tend to have a great deal of influence on the purchasing behavior of their families, whether exerted through whining or technical knowledge. In the mobile industry, this segment is either just entering the market for a phone of their own, or they are developing more autonomy over their consumer choices. So Blyk captured them by giving them what they want (minutes) at the right price (free, to them), and selling a small portion of their time to the advertisers. Blyk created enough interest in mobile advertising that it was able to sell off its mobile network business in 2009—an effort it reportedly launched in order to create a proof of concept for carriers—to concentrate on its core competency of delivering mobile advertising for major carriers, such as O2 in the UK.[3]

An ad-supported option within a tiered pricing structure is also elevating Swedish music streaming site Spotify. In October 2008, Spotify launched in eight European countries with a streaming music service that offers unlimited access to a large catalog of music. The service is supported for the majority of its listeners through twenty seconds of advertising per half hour of music. Alternatively, listeners can opt to pay a ten-euro monthly fee for a "premium" ad-free version. In twelve months, Spotify has amassed 11 million unique users per month, including two hundred fifty thousand paying subscribers.

Listeners who want the ad-supported version now have to be invited by a current user and languish on a waiting list, but you can begin using Spotify right away if you are willing to pay. Spotify has become so popular that Oxford University reportedly banned its use from university networks, saying the system could not handle the high bandwidth.[4]

Like Blyk, Spotify has an advantage over incumbent providers in that it has no legacy customer base to protect. The advertising revenues it earns do not need to make up for lost sales elsewhere in the value chain. Spotify is also motivated to keep the advertising burden low in order to amass an audience over the short term. Fortunately, Spotify is operating in a market for which there is a great deal of projected demand. Respondents to IBM's 2010 Digital Consumer Survey show a 2-to-1 preference for streaming music over downloads—in other words, music as a service rather than music ownership.[5] That same research shows music streaming as an attractive alternative to piracy for Kool Kids. The ad-supported version is free to them and gives them faster access to more song variety than they can easily get from file sharing.

Blyk and Spotify are just two recent examples of new entrants employing payer innovation in apparently saturated and mature markets. Their success suggests that payer innovation can be an attractive path to new revenue streams.

Ad-Supported Revenue Models

Since the advent of the first pamphlets and newspapers, sales of advertising space have been a major driver of revenues in traditional media. Even beyond media, advertising is ubiquitous. On the skyline and in the living room, ad revenues support the operations of entities as diverse as Google and the New York City Metropolitan Transportation Authority, operator of the largest public transportation network in the United States.

Before delving into the details of ad-supported revenue models, it's important to understand just a bit about the massive changes occurring in the business of advertising. On top of a dramatic downturn in spending that goes hand in hand with a recession, the technology of advertising has been in constant upheaval since the advent of the Web banner ad. Interactive ads not only offer a range of new venues for advertising; they also offer unprecedented feedback and tracking possibilities. Advertisers now finally have a glimpse of which half of their dollar is wasted.

By 2013, digital advertising formats—such as Internet banners and search advertising, advertising on cellular phones, messaging through social media sites like Facebook and MySpace, and digital signage that includes messaging in doctors' offices, on elevators, and in taxicabs—are expected to take close to 20 percent share of total advertising dollars, up from 12 percent in 2008.[6]

The changes wrought by the shift to digital advertising create opportunities to apply payer innovation in many industries. One of the major reasons that people tend to hate ads (and have often viewed ad-supported models in nontraditionally advertising-driven industries as a bit tawdry) is their irrelevance.

Taking advantage of the real-time nature of digital formats to make ad design and presentation more relevant to target audiences will help overcome these biases and potentially open new revenue streams.

New Models Move the Industry Beyond Advertising

Advertisers are slowly shifting away from the one-to-many, interruptive advertising model of pre-Internet days. New advertising is more *targeted* to the user's preferences and context; better *integrated* into what she is doing so as to catch her when she is most open to making a purchase; and more or less independent of the *device* she is viewing, whether it is a television, a computer screen, a smartphone, a digital reader, or whatever else comes along. Consumers also have more control over when, how, and even *if* they view ad material.

The targeted, integrated, device-independent, and consumer-controlled future of advertising is so different from the past that it's virtually a whole different beast, and perhaps deserves another name. Regardless, beyond advertising in the "spray and pray" model, we'll find messages shaped to the customer's tastes and integrated into the larger experience with the product. In fact, some of the lost revenue from advertising is already shifting to nonadvertising marketing budgets.[7]

Many of the current experiments along these lines focus on only one of the three trends of targeting, integration, or device. For instance, Hulu is aiming at the device aspect. Hulu content comes from NBC, ABC, and Fox (its owners), and it was supported at launch by commercial spots, just like traditional television. But the commercials are shorter and there are far fewer of them. A sixty-minute broadcast television show may contain sixteen commercials over a total of eight minutes of airtime. On Hulu, the same show might have only four minutes or less of commercials. In 2009, one analyst estimated that a show watched on Hulu earned only one-fifth per thousand viewers what it would have gained from TV broadcast. Yet it seems that earning ad revenue on par with the television channel was not Hulu's first priority.[8] Instead, Hulu was focusing on aggregating an audience. Once it proved it could draw audiences from all over the Web—and compete for views with YouTube—it could focus on monetization. That latter stage seems to have arrived: by October 2009, the site had sold out its inventory on the back of the new prime-time season, and rumors began swirling that the site would add a pay model sometime in the following year. By June 2010, the rumors of pay structures were confirmed as Hulu announced a monthly subscription service which gave users access to more content, along with additional plans to make Hulu content available on the Apple iPad and the Microsoft Xbox.[9]

Integrating the ad into the customer's experience is one area where nonmedia companies are getting a leg up. Walmart, for instance, offers an early and simple model for integrating the ad into the situation of the customer through sales of in-store and online ad space to third parties. Since 2002 the company has peppered its stores with televisions running a loop of product advertising. By some estimates, the 2004 audience for those ads rivaled that of *American Idol*.[10] The company's online property is likewise rich with banner ads for third-party products, from the Nutrisystem weight loss program to Avis car rental.

With the economic downturn, Walmart intensified these efforts to build third-party ad sales into its revenue model. The success of such ventures is a double win for Walmart. Not only does it earn additional revenue from the ad sales, but it also earns retail revenue when an ad convinces a customer to buy a product from Walmart stores.

Ads shown in the store or on Walmart.com may have more traction with Walmart customers than ads geared to a mass audience and slotted between the chopping and caramelizing on *Iron Chef* because they are more integrated. After all, customers wandering around with a shopping cart, whether literally or virtually, are already in the mind-set to buy. A customer researching treadmills on January 2 may be more likely to click on an ad for a discounted Weight Watchers membership simply because she is already thinking about ways to put money toward her weight loss goal.

Another nontraditional player taking advantage of ad revenue opportunities is the New York City taxi industry, whose approach is leveraging location data for better targeting. This payer innovation evolved mostly by accident. An effort that began simply as a way to ensure that riders could easily and securely pay via credit cards ended by putting a full-fledged media device in every Yellow Cab in New York City. Today, along with credit card readers, cabs have display screens and GPS devices. The screens broadcast ads, other content, and real-time maps. The system is synced with the driver's dispatch system, so the device has information on the trip itinerary and can use it to feed ads for restaurants or shops near the rider's final destination.

Blyk goes even further to target its ad content to the user. When a user signs up for a Blyk-enabled service, she must fill out a questionnaire about her likes, dislikes, and activities. This information is then used to define advertising content in those six-times-a-day advertising slots. A Blyk user who says she is an avid runner is not likely to gets ads for fast-food restaurants, but she might get ads for sports apparel or for the newest fitness studio. This is certainly not finely targeted advertising, but the relevance factor increases significantly. The increase in relevance is probably part of the reason why Blyk has registered a 25 percent response rate on its advertising segments.[11]

Twenty-five percent is insanely high in the traditional advertising world. Even if this number drops to half or less of its initial level, it will still blow away the 1 to 2 percent response rate of direct mail promotions, let alone the 0.1 percent click-through for Web advertisements. Indeed, Blyk's advertising response rate is its value proposition to the advertisers that are the source of its revenue.

Interestingly, Blyk customers do not seem to have any problem providing the kind of personal information needed to make advertisements more relevant. IBM consumer research shows that 55 percent of digital consumers—65 percent of the Kool Kids—are willing to provide personal information to marketers in exchange for a concrete benefit. For some, that benefit comes in the form of free airtime on the phone; for others it is a free movie or download; still others see value in loyalty points or discounts. The trick is to understand what consumers value and ensure they see a worthwhile trade-off for their personal information.

Companies outside of media have gained from this balance between information and benefit. Progressive Insurance, for example, launched an experiment in Houston, Texas, more than a decade ago in which it offered drivers the opportunity to pay less for auto insurance if they were willing to provide more information. The information Progressive sought was driving behavior derived from a GPS system the insurer installed in the car. Progressive wanted to create finer pricing options for drivers based on level of risk. Progressive found that customers were willing to give information if they saw value—in this case, from cost savings. The insurer has since rolled the program out to thirteen states, and car insurer Aviva and its sister insurer Norwich Union have launched similar "Pay As You Drive" programs in Canada and the United Kingdom, respectively.[12]

And Now, a Word from Our Sponsor: Fee-Based Indirect Revenues

Product placement and content sponsorship have been a big part of media's revenue model since companies like Alcoa or Procter & Gamble (P&G) financed popular programs such as Edward R. Murrow's *See It Now* or *Candid Camera*. Those shows ran uninterrupted, but the sponsor got a segment at the end to promote its product, or stars would use the product on camera, as Lucille Ball did with P&G's Cheer laundry detergent in an iconic *I Love Lucy* episode.

Today, product placement and sponsorship is everywhere from the lowly can of Coke resident on Simon Cowell's desk during episodes of *American Idol*, to the "brewed by Starbucks" tagline on MSNBC's *Morning Joe*, to the Aston Martins and BMWs driven by James Bond. Sponsorship even has a new twist.

The 2009 George Clooney film *Up in the Air* prominently features American Airlines and Hilton Hotels. Though neither company paid official sponsorship fees, they did let Paramount film in terminals, planes, and hotel rooms free of charge—a significant savings.[13]

The largest revenues from sponsorship are being garnered in the sports industry—of athletes as well as venues, leagues, and specific events. For the Beijing Olympics, corporate giants like Coca-Cola and Lenovo paid an average $72 million for the privilege of sponsoring the Games.[14] The model is so well established, it can be turned to charitable purposes. FC Barcelona, one of the world's most popular soccer teams, is "sponsored" by UNICEF. The space on team jerseys normally reserved for corporate logos bears UNICEF's name, a donation of advertising space worth tens of millions per year. Sports and media are not the only beneficiaries of fee-based indirect revenue models: sponsorship is also the revenue model for most business conferences, as attendees are rarely willing to pay the true cost of putting on the conference.

Sponsorship and product placement are closely related to advertising, and so those models are also under pressure from a concurrent drop in spending. Yet sponsorship done well provides a deeper impression for a product, and not only because sponsors earn prime ad placement. Instead, effective sponsorship creates a stronger connection between sponsor and sponsored than can be achieved just though advertising.

Take athlete sponsorships. It is one thing to see Roger Federer wearing an expensive watch in a *GQ* ad. It is entirely different to see him wearing Nike tennis shoes on the grass courts of

Wimbledon while facing off against Rafael Nadal. The first is creating an association, and a weak one at that, between an admired public figure and a product. The second is showing the product having material impact on the very actions for which we so admire that figure. The message from the latter is, if Roger Federer is wearing Nikes, they must be *really* good.

On the topic of relevance, the music industry has developed a new twist on sponsorship in the past few years in response to the drop in revenues from music sales. Sponsorship of a sort has been the dominant model for the music labels, which sign contracts with artists for a certain number of albums. Particularly with new talent, the label acts as a kind of patron—it finances the artist over a number of years and takes on the expense of marketing and promotion in return for the bulk of revenue from music sales. The problem for the labels is that the traditional contracts between music labels and artists include *only* music sales. Revenue from concert tickets or merchandise was entirely separate—different terms, players, and revenue models. That was not a problem when music sales were high and merchandise sales were essentially a sideshow. But as music sales have tanked and celebrities extend their brand into different entertainment areas, the labels are scrambling to innovate their revenue model and take a piece of every part of the pie.

EMI, for instance, began a new contract with English pop superstar Robbie Williams in 2002 that was one of the first in the industry to take an expansive view of revenue. EMI's deal with Williams reportedly gave him 80 million British pounds to make four albums, the largest contract ever awarded a British star. EMI also committed to helping Williams break into the U.S.

market. In return, Williams was to share part of his revenue from concerts, merchandise, and television.[15]

The deal seemed revolutionary at the time, and something of a coup for the label. After all, artists don't have much incentive to share their nonalbum take. Many feel the labels already get more than their share. So there needs to be clear value from the relationship in order for stars to bite. EMI's promise to make Williams big in the United States seemed to be the deal sweetener, and the failure to make it happen perhaps led to current media reports of Williams's imminent defection from the label.

Eight years later, these 360-degree revenue relationships between labels and artists are still a rarity in the music industry. Yet the model that EMI pioneered may pave the way for a different type of sponsorship in music—and the further demise of the traditional label. Between 2007 and 2009, Live Nation, the largest concert promoter in the United States, signed 360-degree sponsorship contracts with Madonna, U2, and, most recently, Jay-Z. The Jay-Z agreement gave the artist a ten-year, $150 million contract in which the promoter sponsors the artist's recordings, concerts, and entertainment and merchandising activities in exchange for a take of the entire pot. The promise from merchandising alone is significant. Jay-Z's previous nonmusic ventures include a line of clubs and the clothing line Rocawear, which sold in 2007 for $204 million.

Print is also getting into the sponsorship game, with mobile applications. Indeed, the majority of media apps are sold today via sponsorship models rather than being ad-supported. A number of magazine publishers developed specialty versions for the iPhone or the iPod touch, but the launch of the iPad has created a new flurry of activity and experimentation around sponsorship models for mobile apps. For instance, media giant Gannett partnered with sponsor Courtyard by Marriott to launch *USA Today* on the iPad for free to the reader for the first ninety days, after which it converts to a paid subscription.[16] Time Inc. and Condé Nast have similar plans under way for a few of their titles.[17]

Sponsorship Outside of Media

Media isn't the only industry innovating with sponsorship approaches. One current example comes from BabyCenter, a Web site owned by Johnson & Johnson. BabyCenter targets new and expecting mothers, as well as women who are trying to get pregnant, known as TTCs or "trying to conceive" in Webspeak. The site has free information on pregnancy and early-childhood development, as well as expert-moderated forums on topics ranging from infant sleep to toddler discipline.

In a recent innovation, BabyCenter launched a new service called Booty Caller. The service allows TTCs to input data about their monthly cycles. The service will then send a text message to the woman and her partner when she enters the most fertile time of her cycle. The service sponsor? First Response pregnancy tests, a product not owned by J&J (by January 2010, the sponsorship had shifted to E.P.T.).

White Labeling

An outlier in the realm of fee-based third-party revenue is white labeling. White labels conjure for most people thoughts of bottom-shelf, store-brand products that retailers sell at a lower price than brand names. The term itself derives from the music industry—in the days of vinyl, DJs used to cover the labels from their records with white stickers so other DJs couldn't easily copy their playlists. It was a form of revenue protection then. Now it is a form of revenue expansion: white labeling allows product companies to sell their product outside of their traditional market without going out and drumming up demand themselves. Instead, they leverage the audience and demand created by third parties. These models can create wins all around. The product creator can leverage the infrastructure it has built into additional revenue without the cost of customer service or brand building; the customer relationship owner can enhance or extend its relationship with the customer, and the customer gains convenience.

White labeling is still common in retail stores, such as grocery store chains or big-box retailers. Those companies contract with food processors or consumer products manufacturers for such items as low-cost canned vegetables or shampoo. Not every company positions its store brand as the cheap option, though. The President's Choice brand of Canada's Loblaws supermarkets, for instance, is considered high quality, famous for excellent chocolate chip cookies and olive oil.

White labeling is also a common practice in the financial services sector. GE Money, for example, is one of the largest credit card issuers in the United States. Since many of its products are issued through retailers such as Lowe's, the GE logo might not appear at all. For the privilege, retailers pay GE Money a fee to service the cards—print the plastic, process transactions, and, in some cases, carry the debt. Stores manage the relationship with the customer while also placing an ad right in the customer's wallet.

In the digital realm, white-labeled products are more common than many realize. Think back to the early days of the Internet when Expedia first launched as a self-serve travel-booking service. Any shopper who took the initiative to go separately to US Airways or another carrier would have noticed something familiar: the carrier's site looked identical, minus the colors and branding, to Expedia's. Microsoft had effectively sold a white label version of its engine for the carriers to use to service customers who went to them directly.

A more recent, but less ultimately successful, example is Ning, a white-labeled social networking platform provider. The software allowed anyone to create a social network around their field of interest—snowboarding, for example, or cowboy life. Ning was launched with a freemium model. There was a free "cobranded" version that displayed ads automatically; users of the free version could not choose what got presented. Alternatively, there was a fee-based "white label" version of Ning targeted to Web developers and other social site creators who wanted to own and control the advertising space. Ning experienced a great deal of early success. CEO and cofounder Gina Bianchini was featured on the cover of *Fast Company,* and the firm amassed 41 million registered users, with more than double that number visiting Ning-created sites every month, in early 2010.[18] But illustrating the challenge of freemium and advertising-driven revenue models, by April 2010 Bianchini was out, 40 percent of staff was laid off, and the site had killed all of its free offerings, even for existing users. Everyone was forced to start paying at least some direct fees to Ning.[19]

Social Networking

Ning's story is a good entrée to thinking about another form of payer innovation that has been spawned by the success of social networking and other social sites. Initial excitement and interest has been driven just based on the traffic volume and dwell times that social networking sites generate. As of this writing, Facebook has more than 500 million registered users—a pretty compelling audience pool for any advertiser and, in the traditional logic, an advertising moneymaker.

Yet Ning's and Facebook's revenues from straight advertising have been disappointing. The use of the word *monetize* to describe how money will be made from social networking perhaps sums up the problem. Things are monetized—stocks or bonds or grandma's engagement ring. People are . . . well, people. They visit social networking sites to stay in touch with their family members and friends and work connections, not to buy makeup or weight loss aids. Given this context, it is very difficult for advertising on Facebook to be integrated into the experience. Users simply are not in the mind-set to shop. This dissonance likely accounts for the abysmal 0.04 percent average click-through rates on social network sites (the Web as a whole enjoys an average 0.1 percent click-through, and Google achieves 1–2 percent click-through on its search ads).[20]

For Facebook and a few other dominant players, these low click-through rates aren't that much of a cause for concern. The volume of Facebook users means that click-through rates do not need to be very high for the company to earn major money from ads. But the data has quelled some of the initial ardor of people who realize they'll never generate the kind of traffic that Facebook has with a "me-too" social network.

In the wake of that disappointment, though, there is some promise. Facebook's most valuable asset is not necessarily the number of visitors or the time they spend on the site—it's what Facebook knows about its members. Facebook is in a somewhat unique position of having a lot of reliable data about its community of "friends." Users supply huge amounts of personal information. They provide their sex, age, marital status, and sometimes even their address and number of children. They make status updates and respond to what their friends post. Uproar over the company's privacy practices have certainly limited the amount of this information that Facebook can reveal to paying customers, including advertisers, but to date these periodic user revolts seem to be more style than substance. A few months after everyone is up in arms, people are right back where they were—on Facebook divulging lots of data.

For organizations not in the social networking business, the message is certainly not to go start a social network of your own (as the somewhat laughable attempts of some consumer products companies to create social networks around such things as kitty litter have shown). The real opportunity is in thinking about the data your firm accumulates about customers, their behaviors, and their preferences. This information isn't just useful for creating behavioral segments for your own revenue innovation attempts; it's also a potentially high-value asset to others who want either access to your customers (via ads or sponsorships, for instance) or access to your data to improve their own behavioral segmentation. In other words, there may very well be other payers for the value you can deliver to customers via a better understanding of them.

One example of this path being put to work is Twitter. As of mid-2010, Twitter was still growing so fast it was having a hard time keeping up with the traffic. During the final fifteen minutes of the World Cup final, for instance, there were more than two thousand tweets per second.[21] But the real news is that the giant of social communications is turning a profit.[22] The company inked deals with Google and Microsoft to make tweets searchable in late 2009, resulting in $25 million in real revenue, enough to put it in the black for the first time.[23]

Another path to alternative payer revenue streams illustrated by social networks like Facebook is e-commerce integration into other categories. For instance, some social networks and their partners are actively connecting to broader e-commerce activity to earn a cut of the sale from products—real or virtual—advertised or discussed on their pages. One example of this model comes from popular fashion and entertainment magazines *People* (via People.com) and *Lucky*. The magazines have invested in e-commerce engines for their sites, and *People* recently purchased a company called Style Finder, which allows online users to find an outfit or product they see in the magazine's pages and click to purchase it. In a way, they are flipping the equation set by Walmart with its foray into ad sales: where Walmart has moved from commerce to ad publishing, these ad publishers are moving into commerce.

Facebook similarly earns a small slice from any commercial transaction it enables (primarily "virtual goods" to date). But there is a lot of room for that revenue stream to expand. For example, there are applications today that allow a shopper to connect her Facebook network to certain retailers so the friends can give the thumbs up or down on a dress or a pair of shoes. Research shows that a person's inner network can affect whether she completes the sale or not.[24] Right now Facebook is not directly benefiting from these connections, but I expect we will soon see it develop a link to a group of key vendor partners so that users can complete the transaction on Facebook and so earn the social network a slice of the revenue.

Foursquare offers another interesting example of revenue generation from user knowledge. This location-based mobile social networking site allows participants to update their status and let the people they are linked to know where they are—at a bar, at a restaurant, on vacation. Foursquare connects the location information via GPS technology to sponsors that can send the consumers time-limited mobile coupons or discount offers.

Seeing the strength behind the Foursquare model, Facebook has developed its own location-based social network service, branded Facebook Places. Facebook competes with players already in this space by offering prizes or credits when a user checks in, an incentive that has already encouraged users to drive past a store or sit in the parking lot in order to generate a "fake" check-in (though firms like Shopkick are trying to make check-ins more useful to retailers by ensuring the user must enter the physical store to check-in). Still, Facebook Places automatically generates a Facebook page for any establishment the first time a user checks in there. Love it or hate it, those business pages are bound to convert into a huge commerce opportunity in the near future, not to mention the default advertising it creates for the business.

Facebook is not alone among big players in developing location-driven social media. Google has also jumped on that bandwagon with a location-focused service that offers reviews of different restaurants, stores, spas and other providers, an approach very much in keeping with its core search business and famous site ranking. Facebook and Google are both prettying the picture by adding sticky applications such as games, so the check-in becomes just another way of increasing users' dwell time and thereby increases advertising revenues.

Facebook and Google have an advantage in this market given their established user bases. But you should not overlook the niche location-based social network providers, which are building their own user base through social games and social commerce. SCVNGR offers an example of the former with its "Help Vince" scavenger hunt, launched in the summer of 2010. "Help Vince" invites New England Patriots fans to help football star Vince Wilfork find his "lost" Super Bowl ring through various location-based challenges and treks.

Then there are social commerce service providers Groupon and LivingSocial, which offer another twist on payer innovation around social media. Both companies provide registered members with information on places or events in their city, and steep discounts off the merchandise or services of specific providers. They vary, however, in the fact that Groupon users do not get the discount unless enough of them sign up for the deal. This approach encourages the social aspect in which friends push friends to take part. LivingSocial puts no requirement on the number of people who must take a deal, but instead encourages the social element by giving users free merchandise if they get a certain number of friends to sign up.

It's possible we are just in the euphoria of early days and that the deals will become less attractive over time, and so draw less participants. Yet I don't think location-based social commerce is a short-term payer innovation. The vendors benefit from these group buying approaches in the guarantee of a certain number of customers, in the case of Groupon, or in guaranteed ad views. The providers are just beginning to gain traction. Groupon recently finished a round of financing that valued the company at $1.2 billion.[25] There are at least another dozen startups around the world with substantial funding in the same space. Add in the fact that Twitter now also tweets a Daily Deal, and it is pretty much foregone that social buying is going to play an enormous role in social media monetization in the coming years.

MomsLikeMe.com takes a different approach. The first version of the site, Indy MomsLikeMe.com, focused on the Indianapolis metro area, was launched in 2007 by the *Indianapolis Star*, a property of the Gannett Company. Gannett is a publisher with holdings in numerous papers, including *USA Today*. Senior executives at the *Star* had known for years that they were not reaching mothers of young children in their distribution area, a potential audience of 180,000 people. With shrinking circulation from its newspaper, the company was looking for new sources of revenue.

A product development team created a social networking site targeted to moms in the Indianapolis area. The site focuses on the local area and a particular demographic—women between the ages of twenty-four and forty-four with children under the age of seventeen—illustrating that while behavioral segments are the future, demographic segments will continue to be important, particularly while you are building a customer base.

Unlike many Web properties launched by newspapers and magazines, Indy MomsLikeMe is light on original content. This serves Gannett fine, since its siloed print properties would likely resist creating content for a separate organization, even one contained within the Gannett family. Indy MomsLikeMe launched as a community-oriented discussion forum that tackles top-of-mind issues for moms in the region. It also has sections for moms to sell secondhand baby gear or find child care or a play group. The site is run by two full-time editorial staff members and a handful of "discussion leaders," local moms paid $25 a week to initiate and participate in site discussions. A "mom squad" also attends local mom-oriented events to promote the site. A monthly *IndyMoms* newspaper is distributed for free through direct mail and magazine racks.

The effort began with the Indianapolis site as well as a parallel initiative for Cincinnati (Cincy MomsLikeMe) and a few other localities. In its first year, Cincy Moms was expected to bring in about $200,000 worth of revenue from advertising and sponsorship opportunities—it made $386,000 after six months.

Early success allowed the initiative to expand into dozens of other localities (there are now more than one hundred) and create a national platform, USA MomsLikeMe.com, from which Gannett can sell advertising and sponsorships for the entire network of sites, as well as for individual cities or clusters. This offers advertisers an immensely attractive proposition, compared with local papers, which sell ad space individually, even when they are part of a larger network, creating a great deal of complexity and frustration for national advertisers.

It should be said that MomsLikeMe is not bringing moms to the Gannett newspapers, nor is it alone stemming the loss in revenue from traditional print properties. Gannett earned $586 million in digital revenues in 2009, but most of that came from its investments in CareerBuilder and ShopLocal.[26] Attrition from the *Indianapolis Star* and papers like it continues apace. New competition is also coming from local, parent-oriented sites such as Nickelodeon's Parents Connect and Go City Kids properties. But Gannett was a first mover in the space, and its initiative shows what is possible with a social network that strikes a chord with an undertargeted audience.

Payer Innovation Pitfalls

The above models and examples offer food for thought for companies that want to test new sources of revenue by shifting who the payer may be for their goods, services, or customer information. Yet eyes tend to roll at the suggestion that anyone can earn robust revenues from advertising today, especially if you're talking to traditional media companies.

This skepticism is justified. Advertising will be difficult to pull off as a sole source of revenue, especially if you are talking about traditional one-to-many advertising. That model will, quite frankly, continue to struggle, especially in analog media markets. It won't be a linear decline, and a bounce-back as the global economy hopefully picks up may hide the overall trend for a while. But make no mistake, traditional advertising is on a long-term decline.

Nor will innovative advertising models like the ones I presented in this chapter offer immediate wins for companies that don't think through their value proposition and match it with a customer need. For every model that seems to be experiencing some success, there is a counterstory of a company that tried and failed to get it right. Home Depot, for example, explored and ultimately abandoned a third-party advertising model like Walmart's. Virgin Mobile had a Blyk-like service called Sugar Mama that awarded customers free minutes when they visited a microsite to watch and rate advertising. Unlike Blyk, which integrates advertising into phone use, Sugar Mama required the user to take the initiative to visit a separate site on her own time. The service folded shortly after launch.

Another pitfall when it comes to selling information to third parties is the very real possibility of transgressing the difficult-to-define, and rapidly changing, written and unwritten rules about privacy. Facebook has, of course, been knocked several times, and regulators the world over are struggling to keep up with consumer behavior and business practices. Any experiments in this area have to build in the very real risk of either alienating customers or having a promising revenue stream shut down by regulatory changes.

Earlier in this chapter, I discussed how advertising is evolving from its interruptive, mass-audience origins into a more targeted, integrated, and device-independent experience. I provided examples of what that targeting looks like in these early stages, from location-based advertising seen in taxicabs or sent via Foursquare to demographic targeting like Cincy Moms and Indy Moms. These examples illustrate that the shift is happening, and I truly believe that in its most sophisticated form, new advertising will allow companies to engage in an ongoing, relevant, and high-value interaction with customers that will benefit both sides.

What these models are not doing is fully making up for lost revenue from traditional channels. This is less of an issue for companies such as Blyk, for which mobile advertising is not replacing traditional advertising. It is, however, an issue for companies like Hulu, which could be accelerating the movement of customers to digital channels from its parent companies' analog channels. For print media or television as well, this is a big challenge.

These examples also make clear that the current implementation of more targeted advertising is not yet all that sophisticated. Advertisers simply lack sufficient information about consumers to improve on the experience. When a server delivers ads to the screen in the back seat of a taxi, it is capitalizing on the fact that it knows *where* the rider is going and *how* he is getting there—but it has no idea *why*. So if I am traveling to New York City's Times Square to see a Broadway play, I may appreciate knowing about some gourmet restaurants in the area; but if I am traveling to New York City's Times Square because my personal trainer works in a gym there, those restaurant ads will likely miss their mark.

If you're going to experiment with payer innovation to generate new revenue streams, you need to be able to deliver highly targeted, context-relevant ads, sponsorship opportunities, or active social networks. That's a big barrier for most companies. In the segmentation chapter, I discussed the challenges that companies have finding meaning in consumer data. Improved intelligence is worth a premium in today's market—Netflix recently paid a $1 million prize in a contest to improve the performance of the recommendation engine that mines its data on customer preferences. Companies with deep pockets throw money at the problem. For everyone else, efforts at using analytics have not delivered to expectations. Most companies are going to need help here.

The challenge of finding meaning in data is exacerbated within traditional companies by the fact that different divisions within the same company often resist sharing what they know. Digital businesses are often incubated in separate units walled off from the traditional core of the company. These walls are difficult to break down once they have been erected.

The challenge that daily newspapers have had navigating between offline customers with paid subscriptions and online, often nonpaying, readers is representative of the problem. Publishers have realized they should offer a somewhat different experience on the Web from what they have in the paper. Blogs, question-and-answer forums, and moderated discussions are all part of the online newspaper experience. But the digital editor is someone other than the print editor, and their content is less than seamless with print. These product managers, in short, are not always aligned, so it is hard for them to share knowledge and help inform revenue models based on what consumers are reading and how that readership could be monetized.

Payer Innovation Lessons

The pitfalls of indirect revenues in the current era bring out a number of lessons that media and nonmedia companies can draw from. The first is to be careful about where you drop your anchor—the anchor price, that is. The Internet has become synonymous with content that is free to the consumer. Yet content is not free to produce, and online advertising is not, in most cases, generating enough revenue to pay for the content creation. When companies charge $0, they are effectively telling the customer that the product is worth nothing—who would ever want to pay even a nominal amount for an item signaled as worthless? So think first before setting an anchor price of zero if your plan involves any direct revenue streams. You may find it is more difficult to migrate customers than you thought.

The second lesson is that few companies will survive on indirect revenues alone. Offering highly targeted opportunities to advertisers or sponsors will dramatically increase your revenue potential, but don't overestimate the total size of the revenue opportunity. Smart companies will look to diversify their revenue models, with indirect models targeted perhaps to one segment of customers, or offered as a complementary revenue source, as Spotify and Hulu are doing with the dual approach of offering ad-supported and paid subscription models. There's more to learn from media here. Although media companies have been most affected by the loss of traditional advertising, they do have a lot of experience in managing multiple revenue models around the same product, as newspapers have done by balancing subscriptions with advertisement and classified revenues. Those skills may be worth acquiring if you're considering an experiment in payer innovation.

The third lesson is to manage conflict between direct and indirect revenue business units, and find a way to tap into the richness of information and experience that these distinct groups can bring. This will require some finesse. A common conflict in the media industry is between ad salespeople, who want to give ads as much prominence as possible in order to attract advertising customers and charge higher rates, and subscription salespeople, who know their customers are interested in dodging advertising as much as possible. There are always challenges to serving two masters.

All of these challenges can be interpreted as very good news for companies that are just beginning with payer innovation. It means there is some time. Everyone is still finding their way. Adopting behavioral segmentation will make it easier to know who you are dealing with at any given time—and potentially allow you to create a revenue stream from the information you base your behavioral segmentation on. If you're outside of media, you probably don't have entrenched relationships with advertisers and creative agencies—an enviable position. You can take advantage of new technologies and emerging models to feed your experiments more easily than those with entrenched models and some barriers to change. It would be wise to avoid committing to any particular technology or model, since the industry is in significant flux and will remain so for the foreseeable future.

Getting Started

Table 3-1 provides a review of payer innovation. What are some of the questions you should ask around strategy, infrastructure, and operations when considering whether to pursue payer innovation?

Strategy

- Do you have the right insights about your consumers in place to offer value to third-party payers?

- Do you have the third-party models in place to enable relevant offers to the consumer?

- Does your advertising strategy offer clear advantage and differentiation for marketers over your competitors?

- Do you understand how your revenues will shift from third-party payers versus directly from consumers in the upcoming years?

Infrastructure

- Do you have the analytics environment in place to enable real-time insights about your consumers' behavior to deliver to third-party payers?

TABLE 3-1

Payer innovation in brief

Model	Traditional mode	Innovation	Digital-era-examples
Ad-supported	One-to-many, interruptive ads designed and delivered for a particular medium	Relevant, integrated, device-independent material, sometimes delivered in markets that have not previously relied on ad models	• Blyk • Spotify • Walmart • NYC taxi
Sponsorship or product placement	Television or live event sponsorship with/or driven by product placement	Associate a brand with new forms of content delivered through new channels in ways more relevant and integrated with the customer's experience	• BabyCenter's "Booty Caller" (P&G and E.P.T., First Response) • EMI/Robbie Williams • Live Nation • Courtyard by Marriott/Gannett on the iPad
White labeling	Revenue protection by hiding product/differentiation	Sell via a third party to customers outside of your direct market	• Ning
Social networking	Word-of-mouth promotion within certain geographies or customer segments	Digitally enable interaction and dialogue within social groups; target social influencers	• *People*/Style Finder • Gannett Moms-LikeMe • Foursquare

- Does your infrastructure allow you to experiment and provide a greater variety of third-party payer models?

- What are you doing to enhance the third-party revenue potential (e.g., providing information in different ways, providing access to information)?

Operations

- Is your organization aligned to deliver a consumercentric third-party payer model, as opposed to siloed offerings based on product or channel as a proxy for reaching the consumer?

- Are you working with the right partners to enable flexibility?

4

Package Innovation

Electronics retailer Best Buy noticed in the late 1990s that returns were skyrocketing. When asked, customers often complained that an item didn't work, but the real issue was often that the customer had installed the software incorrectly or had not connected peripheral devices properly. Customers just weren't up to the task of operating the complex, feature-rich products that earn retailers the highest margins.

Seeing an opportunity to decrease expensive returns, Best Buy bought Geek Squad in 2002. Geek Squad was founded as the layman's technical support desk. The firm was on call to help technology consumers with computer issues (software installation, virus cleaning, migration, network setup, and data backup) and help them figure out how to install and use their electronics.

Part of what made the firm stand out was a willingness to go to customers and provide in-home service.

Best Buy saw the opportunity to integrate Geek Squad's installation and technology coaching services into the initial sale of electronic products, boosting revenue and heading off returns caused by user error. Cutting down on those returns would have a big impact on the retailer's margins. Bundling in Geek Squad was a hit. By 2009, the more than ten thousand Geek Squad division members were making 4 million service calls a year and contributing to the 7 percent of Best Buy's annual revenue from services.[1]

Other device retailers have integrated services with their product-focused business, but none have achieved the same brand recognition as Geek Squad—certainly not the bankrupt Circuit City. *Geek Squad* has become synonymous with anytime technical help. Geek Squad and its reputation for reliability plays a role in Best Buy's leading 21 percent retail market share.

Packaging Value

Best Buy's move into services is an example of *package innovation*, the third revenue innovation approach. Package innovation involves competing more broadly across the value chain by changing what you sell—not the products per se, but what exactly the customer pays for. What's in the package, in other words. Package innovation takes three main forms: componentization, value integration, and value extensions (see figure 4-1).

The form of package innovation most intimately connected to the Internet and digital products is *componentization,* or the

FIGURE 4-1

Package innovation models

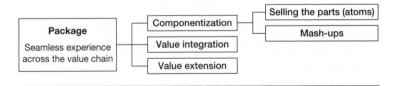

splitting of existing products into smaller component parts that can be monetized in a different form for different use. Once products can be split, they can also be reassembled in a different form, as with *mash-ups*—a term that describes bringing parts of two different products or services together to create a new value proposition.

Value integration involves looking for up- or downstream opportunities within the same value chain. Best Buy's acquisition of Geek Squad is a value integration of services to a product-focused retailer. Such product-to-service moves have a long history in technology and manufacturing, where leasing and service contracts have been a part of the industry for many decades. Package innovation via value integration today shows companies moving in any direction, from products to services, services to products, or creating custom mixes of products and services from several different sources.

Value integration usually takes place within the same value chain. *Value extensions*, however, allow companies to expand their brand or product into adjacent markets. Popular in the entertainment industry with the extension of personality-driven brands— like Oprah Winfrey, Martha Stewart, and, more recently, Tyra Banks—value extension allows companies to leverage marketing power into parallel areas.

As the examples of this chapter attest, the point of package innovation is to breathe new life and purpose into an existing resource. You may innovate by selling an existing product or part of a product into a new market, or by taking a part or product from elsewhere in the value chain and integrating it with your core business. Package innovation as a revenue innovation does not go so far as the deeper business model innovation approaches of enterprise or industry innovations referred to in the introduction. Revenue innovation is not about shifting away from your core revenue source, but driving incremental revenue shifts, and so package innovations are more about integrating or adding value from elsewhere in the value chain as a value-add to the company's core proposition.

Package innovations can be fuzzy and hard to define, largely because their nature is to shape-shift from one thing into another. Innovations can also straddle a few models and even shift depending on perspective—one company may componentize its product, which is then taken up to create value integration for another. The precise definitions, in short, are less important than finding new avenues for revenue growth.

Componentization

Componentization involves cutting an existing product into its component parts, which may be sold for a different purpose and/or into a new customer segment, though they may also just be a better fit for existing customers. Componentization in some ways has a longer history outside of media than within. For example, the software industry has gone through repeated cycles of stand-alone programs that get bundled into suites, only to be componentized and bundled again. Enterprise software vendor SAP, for instance, sells traditional finance and human resource components, as well as additional components for operations or business processes (benefits management and so on).

Componentization also appears in unlikely industries—hospitality, to name one. The Four Seasons hotel chain continues to create a specific environment and ambience for customers in the hotels, but it also sells components of the "experience" for customers to enjoy wherever they happen to be. You can still buy the traditional package by booking a room for $400 or more a night. Or you can buy the component by purchasing the mattress or the linens or the bathrobe and slippers to have at home.

There are lessons to be learned from the media industry on using componentization as a revenue innovation, especially given that digital formats allow for an almost unlimited variety of components, sliced and delivered with relative ease to the particular needs of an individual. In the most interesting models, the component is used for a different purpose or function than the original. This approach has the added benefit of creating a new market without risk of cannibalizing the old. For instance, commercial content uploaded onto YouTube often comes in snippets that last a few minutes—a favorite skit or blooper—rather than an entire episode. Those snippets are increasingly matched with advertising content.

The most compelling componentization story in terms of revenue comes from music. Prior to digitization, music componentization happened in niche, ad hoc ways. Music publishers took advantage of opportunities to sell song rights for use in films or commercials, but the film producer often used only part of the song—the chorus or a bridge, for example—to create a marketing association or hook.

Componentization in music has since taken on a different scale of automation and profitability with the ringtone. Ring-tones came into the market in 1997, when teenagers in Japan replaced the generic ring patterns on their mobile phones with snippets of real songs. In 1998 a ringtone "book" was published in Japan, allowing users to easily integrate song snippets into their phones.

The rest of the world soon followed Japan's lead. Ringtone sales reached $2 billion worldwide in 2004 on account of mass downloads of twenty-second song splices at around $2 each. Interestingly, in some places the twenty-second ringtone is more popular than the song itself—in 2004 in South Korea, ringtone sales exceeded sales for singles.[2]

While ringtones capture the revenue potential of componen-tizing, they also show how quickly markets turn. Off its 2004 height, the ringtone market is in rapid decline. Just as in so many other areas, technology overtook the revenue model. Today it's relatively easy to cut an MP3 into whatever length you want and load it onto your smartphone. In fact, many smartphones sim-ply let you pick any audio file as your ringtone.

Componentization is on the upswing in other sectors, such as video games. The Star Wars franchise has a series of video games, and recently launched *Star Wars: The Clone Wars Game Creator* under the umbrella of the Cartoon Network Digital. The game creator is a site that allows gamers to create their own Star Wars games out of componentized parts. In this instance, players design a racing/action game using Star Wars characters and vehicles. They then lay out the race course, including obstacles and other objectives (like destroying an enemy base). Gamers can then upload their created games to the community site for others to play and ultimately for users to vote on the best creation. Previous efforts along these lines include the *Ben 10: Alien Force Game Creator*, which the Cartoon Network claims as one of the most popular interactive games on the site.[3]

Componentized services have also become a revenue generator for a number of companies. Perhaps the best example is Amazon, which has broken out some of the internal services it has developed to drive its core business model and begun selling those services to others. For instance, Amazon now generates revenues as a cloud computing provider by selling server capacity in its data centers. It also has been moving into payment management services. Any site can now offer Amazon's "1-Click" buying—for a fee, of course. Amazon developed these services in order to drive its main revenue-generating business, not to offer them as products in their own right. But by employing componentization, it has created a package innovation, and new revenue, around a core in-house resource. (See "Components, Platforms, and Add-ons.")

Companies can also componentize a particular in-house skill set for package innovation. For example, the success of Apple's brick-and-mortar Apple Store has attracted the attention of other brands: in 2009 Disney began working with Steve Jobs and his retail experts to redesign Disney stores along the lines of the super-successful Apple stores.[4]

Components, Platforms, and Add-ons

Companies like Apple, Microsoft, Twitter, and Amazon have attacked componentization from a different angle—not by splitting up their own products, but by opening them up enough to allow others to write or develop add-on components. Effectively, they position their products as platforms and allow the broader market to improve the value.

The iPhone App Store is the best-known example. From financial planning tools and personal fitness programs to mapping functions and video games, there is an iPhone app for nearly every need, created through the initiative and creativity of third parties. From a revenue innovation perspective, the important part is that Apple takes a 30 percent cut of each app sold. While the apps are generally very low cost, the huge number of app purchases generates substantial revenue in aggregate.[a] Of course, the real money is still in the sales of iPhones, iPod touch devices, and iPads, but Apple has innovated a new revenue stream that also helps drive sales of its profitable devices.

Apple did not write the book on this approach. Microsoft may be the company most skilled at getting others to improve the usefulness of its products. Bill Gates realized decades ago that Windows could only take off on the

Mash-ups

Once a product is split into component parts, those parts can be reassembled and laid over each other to create a new product known as a mash-up. Mash-ups originally came out of the music industry when DJs took pieces from two unrelated songs desktop and the server if the applications that individuals and companies wanted to use were available on Windows. So the company makes it as easy as it can for independent software vendors to develop Windows-based applications. It offers training and certification, and publishes application programming interfaces (APIs) and toolkits. Microsoft even develops industry-specific packages of prebuilt programs. A lot of coding still needs to be done around them, but Microsoft takes care of the basics. Where Apple innovated right past Microsoft was in figuring out how to generate revenue from the work of all those independent software coders without buying their companies.

The platform model of componentization is spreading fast. Google is clearly following in Apple's footsteps by promoting the Android as a multipurpose device operating system complemented by the Android app store, where developers can sell their products. The cellular telecom companies are trying to follow along as well. Amazon is positioning the Kindle as a platform, and content as components. Both Twitter and Facebook are attempting to use their APIs and authentication services as platforms that can bring them additional revenue streams.

[a] The iTunes Store generated an estimated $4 billion in 2009, according to the Dataquest report *The Revenue Opportunity Beyond the Hype,* December 2009.

(some of the earliest involved mixing rap lyrics with Beatles songs, and vice versa) and combined them to create something new. These early mash-ups proved such a hit that the form was quickly adopted by both the labels and fans.

Web programmers quickly got into the act and turned to making mash-ups using Web services and data from a variety of places. This has led to an explosion of single-purpose Web applications that, for instance, use Google's mapping services with government data to track U.S. government spending.

The larger concept of mixing two previously unrelated products offers some unusual possibilities outside of media. A German company has a service called Vessel Tracker that integrates Google Earth with port and ship data to track the location of any registered oceangoing vessel in the world. That makes it tremendously useful to logistics managers and shipping brokers, who dramatically strengthen their hands in negotiating by knowing how much cargo capacity is anchored outside Singapore or on its way to San Francisco. The site also uses advertising to generate an additional revenue stream from free users, who have access to only limited data.

The key to package innovation via mash-ups is relinquishing control over a valuable asset. That asset may be services that you provide, or it can be data that you capture. You gain revenue by charging those who use your asset in their mash-ups—or by creating your own mash-ups from others' assets. As always, there is some risk in allowing access to your assets or information. One humorous example comes from the site Please Rob Me, which grabs data from Twitter and Foursquare (a location-sharing service) and highlights people who are broadcasting their "not at home" status. Since many Twitter users use their real names, the site offers a thought exercise in how an intelligent thief could use just a few bits of information to identify low-risk opportunities to break into people's homes.

Value Integration

Componentization and mash-ups require companies to divide the existing product into parts for different user groups. Value integration allows them to reconsider or expand where they bring value to the same customers in the value chain. That can take the form of adding a services component to a product or adding products to services.

Value integration models very overtly allow companies to capitalize on revenue opportunities that exist elsewhere within the value chain. Integration recognizes that the dominant consumer need or desire in any value chain is fluid—the power holder today may be a loss leader tomorrow.

Music again offers a particularly pointed example of how quickly these dynamics change. I have mentioned that the value in music has shifted since 2006 to other parts of the value chain. The compound annual growth rate (CAGR) for content was –2 percent between 2003 and 2007, but the music industry as a whole grew during that time on the back of device sales and music promotion revenues from live performances and sponsorships (see figure 4-2). In effect, the real innovators in music may be device manufacturers like Apple, which integrated device sales, music purchases, and music cataloging and organization into an easy and seamless experience. Promoters are also innovating, as I discussed in the section on sponsorship in chapter 3. For their part, music labels and retailers are now scrambling to ink deals that give them a cut of the other parts of the value chain, but in most instances they are relying on the largesse of the artist, not on their own innovation. The lesson

FIGURE 4-2

Music industry growth shifts to other parts of the value chain

2003–2007 industry CAGR: 3%

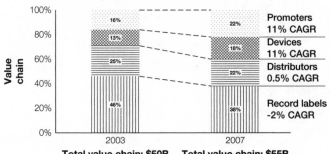

Total value chain: $50B   Total value chain: $55B

Sources: PWC Global Outlook 2008–2012; CEA Market Research 2008; Veronis Suhler 2007; eMarketer 2007; and IBM analysis.

from music is to look for opportunities to integrate value into your product before value shifts force you to it. Fortunately, there are a number of successful cases on how to do it.

"Service-ization," or turning a product into a service via leasing or service fees, is one approach to value integration that has been a staple of manufacturers of capital equipment like GE. Software vendors have also long packaged a service element into their products with the typical 8 to 12 percent they add to licenses for maintenance, incremental version upgrades, and troubleshooting. More recently, vendors have innovated the package with "software as a service" (SaaS) models. SaaS vendors wrap the network and hardware maintenance into service offerings by owning and hosting the software, hardware, and network in-house. The user pays more for the license but is spared the variable cost of ownership of hardware and network management.

In a more offbeat vein, the Interface flooring company offers a services program for commercial carpeting. A few years ago, Interface, a leading manufacturer of carpet tiles, developed ways to recycle both the backing glue for carpet, as well as the two types of nylon fiber typically used to manufacture the tiles— nylon 6 and nylon 6.6. These innovations meant that Interface now had a way to keep its products out of landfills, a major development. But it needed a way to get the carpet back after use.

Enter the service agreement. Carpet comes in rolls or tiles, and most commercial installations use tiles that are sold outright and replaced every few years. Tiles placed along walking routes get all the wear, though, whereas the tiles placed under furniture and equipment stay pristine—that's, say, a 30–70 split between used tile and good tile over a three- to five-year period. The Interface leasing option allows companies to replace only the tiles that are worn out during the life of the lease. The user saves money, and Interface gets its product back to push through the recycling process (which has the benefit of dramatically cutting the cost of producing new tiles).

Value integration through service contracts is a way for manufacturers to improve customer loyalty and more firmly embed a product in the customer's business. Interface's approach goes further to take on more of the product life cycle. In a way, the Interface solution is for the corporate equivalent of the Massive Passive. Rather than require the client to set and act on their own preferences around implementation, use, retirement, and disposal of assets, Interface takes care of it for them. Industrial lubricant manufacturer Castrol does something similar with Castrol Complete, a service offering that includes, with the sale of the lubricants, a range of services around employee training, regulatory compliance, and end-of-life disposal or re-refining. In our environmentally conscious age, service models such as Interface's and Castrol's allow manufacturers to more easily comply with safe-disposal laws, since they get the product back at the end of its useful life and can track where the materials go. As an added bonus, these companies are redesigning their products in such a way that they can reuse materials they get back and lower their input costs.

Service elements also work to capitalize on new opportunities, as Best Buy has done with Geek Squad. Geek Squad is a necessary service because the increased variety in consumer technology makes Geeks necessary. A generation ago, only people who could teach themselves how to use them bought high-tech products. It was akin to my father teaching himself the basics of car repair—every car owner simply knew how to change his own oil and replace a flat. Today roadside service is a big business because few people are willing to spend the time (or physical effort) to learn how to perform such relatively simple tasks as changing a tire.

Another example of value integration comes from the developing world. C. K. Prahalad's research on the "bottom of the pyramid" catalyzed many global firms, particularly in consumer goods, to begin looking for ways to access the growing consumer market in India, Latin America, and Africa. Given how fragmented those markets are and how difficult it is to build a distribution network, many companies have found it slow going. A few, though, like Unilever, have begun experimenting with harnessing the networks built by microfinance institutions.

These networks allow microfinance providers to reach into poor communities profitably—as well as have a very good idea of the community members that are raising their incomes. That makes them the perfect distribution network for consumer goods that microfinance customers may now have the means to purchase.[5]

Value Integration in Media: Creative Advertising

Value integration also plays a role in media. Magazine publishers are leveraging the creative talent they have on staff to offer creative services directly to advertisers. At a time when magazine advertising page sales have declined by 28 percent, and creative advertising firms, such as holding company WPP, are trying to diversify beyond their creative businesses, a few major players in the magazine industry are taking the in-house talent formerly responsible for the magazine's visuals and layout, and using them to develop campaigns for advertising partners.[6] Recall from the chapter on payer innovation that advertisers are beginning to demand more relevant advertising opportunities? By doing the creative work in-house, the magazine is better able to design the ad to align with the content of the magazine. Hearst and Condé Nast are first movers in this area.

In October 2009, Hearst published across its properties a series of in-house-designed ads for the electronics brand LG. The ad for *House Beautiful* focused on kitchen appliances; the ad in *Cosmopolitan*, on text messaging via LG smartphones. Each print ad had a corresponding micro Web site, useful for engaging the reader through a different medium and for tracking the ad's engagement impact.

Condé Nast similarly added creative services to ad sales for the promotion of the new Lexus HS 250h in October 2009. The publisher recruited three different teams of well-known artists and designers to create distinct car ads to fit with the content of a number of its titles (*Wired,* the *New Yorker, Vogue, Vanity Fair, GQ, Architectural Digest*).[7] In neither case is Condé Nast or Hearst moving away from its core business of publishing. Offering creative services is simply an additional revenue stream developed in parallel for an elite set of advertising customers.

Analytics as an Ad Service

Publishing's integration of creative services is arguably only a first-round effort in a broader trend of media players offering add-on services to former transactional sales of ad space. The digital realm is also jumping into the act. Google, for example, is increasingly making its analytics services available to advertisers as a sweetener to induce more ad spending.

Google's core search business has long earned revenues through sales of ad space via "search word" auctions. Google's analytics capability then allows the company to track the response that searchers have to the advertisements. Google knows how many people are clicking and whether anything makes them more likely to click or not (a certain combination of search words, for example, or the time of day). This same intelligence has allowed the company to improve the quality of its search results by placing those links that customers engage with higher up the list than the ones that get a tepid response.

Google is now applying that same analytics intelligence to the video clips on YouTube. Through its "Content ID" technology,

Google tags some clips and tracks their popularity and usage. This ultimately earns Google more advertising revenue—since it knows where to place the commercial—and it helps media companies better understand how people consume their content.

Commercial video advertising on YouTube is still new and marks a major change. Even now when a clip of a professionally produced movie or show appears on YouTube, the content owner asks the site to take the clip down. But that is and continues to be something of a moving target, given how little control Google has over users posting different versions of the same snippet.[8] Over time, many media companies have given in to the inevitable reality of content repurposing and shifted their approach to monetize the clips and share in the ad revenue.

So Google now puts advertising in some content on YouTube (different from the pop-up, semitransparent ads that appear on most videos). And it has analytics to show how many views a particular clip receives, whether the clip is watched in whole or in part, and where people tend to abandon it or rewind it to watch again. Google passes this analytics information on to the content owner as a free add-on rather than as a paid service. It is betting that advertisers, armed with in-depth information about what consumers like, will respond with more, and more finely tuned, ad placements, resulting in more money for YouTube/Google. The analytics could also be used to inform product development at the advertiser, creating further lock-in.

This can only be the beginning for Google. YouTube's high bandwidth costs most definitely do not come for free. So there is going to be a lot more revenue innovation coming from Google as it chases revenue streams by creating different packages of the service, the audience, its analytics capability, and its ad technology. For students of revenue innovation, Google/YouTube is definitely one to watch.

Value Integration Through Product Redefinition

Currently, Google's analytics are used to make the real product, advertising, more valuable. Yet the integration of information into products that have traditionally been sold through transactional one-and-done formats is opening the door for a different kind of customer—and revenue—relationship, one that may cause companies to rethink and reprice the various parts of what they sell. In the auto industry, the presentation of information to the driver in real time about his location, speed, energy consumption, or even, in the case of theft, the location of his car could begin to provide a significant portion of a vehicle's overall profit. GM's OnStar and Ford's Sync are early examples of these kinds of services. Visionaries in the utilities sector are likewise talking about the future "smart home," in which smart sensors hooked up to appliances do more than just monitor energy use. The smart washing machine may sense the mix of fabrics in the cycle and adjust the water temperature, or the smart refrigerator may keep track of the food inventory and notify the shopper of the house when it's time to buy milk.

These ideas will become reality only for industries that are successfully able to shift the customer's understanding of what he is paying for. I already mentioned the electric car company Better Place, the aim of which is to make electric cars commonplace on the world's roads. To achieve that goal, founder Shai Agassi believes the cars need to be priced so low that the driver does not need to think about the decision to drive electric. Within such a low-margin model, the automaker needs to get its revenue somewhere else—by earning services revenue from battery switching and charging stations, for example.[9]

In that context, I think the auto industry missed a huge opportunity following the brouhaha over reports of unintended acceleration in Toyotas. Though those reports have now largely been discredited—a very small number of drivers experienced actual problems with sticky pedals and floor mats; the majority of problems were caused by drivers pushing the wrong pedal—for a time there was a push for regulations to require automakers to install much more sophisticated black boxes in vehicles. While doing so would prove initially costly, if automakers were forced to do so by regulation, prices would rise across the board, limiting the damage to any one manufacturer. More importantly, the sophisticated black boxes would open the possibility for whole new high-margin service packages. Imagine if you could subscribe to a service that told you exactly when to change your oil (and what type to use) based on your driving patterns, or one that gave you daily tips on how to maximize fuel efficiency? And of course, such data would open the door to other pricing and payer innovations as well.

Nespresso offers a current example of product redefinition in the coffee industry by selling and pricing all parts of the value chain. Typically, providers in the coffee beverage sector are either device manufacturers that sell the razor (i.e., the coffee machine) or food processors that sell the blades (i.e., the coffee).

Nespresso does both. The Nestlé-owned coffee company sells specialty, easy-to-use espresso machines designed to work only with its proprietary "pod" coffees, a model that has become hugely popular for office, hotel, restaurant, and, increasingly, home environments. And unlike other razor/blade models, in which one side is priced as a loss leader and opened to outside providers, Nespresso keeps its system closed, with all parts of its value proposition priced at a premium. An eight-ounce Nespresso cappuccino costs twice as much as the same size drink made from pod coffee competitors K-Cups or Coffee Pod, but despite these high prices, the company grew by 40 percent in 2007, exceeding the industry growth by 5 percentage points and earning it close to 27 percent of the worldwide espresso machine market share in 2010.[10]

Value Extensions

Value integration involves adding new services or products within an existing value chain to create new packages. A related approach to package innovation comes from extending one's brand or product line to offer new value in parallel markets, and ultimately offering new packages in that market based on the ability to straddle two sectors. There are dozens of examples of value extensions among the famous. Celebrity—or at least notoriety—generates a lot of buzz, enough to allow Gwen Stefani and Sean Combs to create clothing lines; Jennifer Lopez, a fragrance; and Gwyneth Paltrow to do whatever it is that GOOP does. Professional homemaker Martha Stewart has her fingers in even more pots, from her talk show, to her magazine, to her line of linens and cutlery and carpets. Her fame cannot be stopped—not even by jail time.

Tyra Banks is now fiercely getting into the act. The onetime supermodel first parlayed her knowledge and experience of the modeling world to launch her own reality TV show, *America's Next Top Model*, before adding her own *Tyra Show* talk show and the one-season wonder *Stylista*, another reality effort for aspiring fashion editors. From the first two shows, Banks is reported to have earned $18 million a year—not bad for a former teen model.[11]

As these examples attest, it seems more natural to extend a brand that is strong and positively received, particularly when the target markets are populated by the same—or similarly accessible—segments. But what happens with brands that have negative associations?

Take Nike. Though it is one of the most famous sports shoe and apparel brands in the world, it has come under fire in the past for inhumane and toxic conditions in the factories where the shoes are made. Like many manufacturers, Nike designs and markets its products, but it leaves production and manufacturing to channel partners in low-wage countries (Vietnam and Indonesia, most famously). The production facilities are not always paying workers the going wage, respecting minimum-age restrictions, keeping reasonable hours, or maintaining a safe working environment. Nike has been nabbed numerous times in the past two decades for the environmental and humanitarian missteps of its manufacturing partners. In certain circles, the brand is associated with profit at the expense of the people who make the products.

In contrast, there is Converse, maker of those 1980s-style "Chuck Taylor" sneakers that were once the required footwear of the punk scene. Converse shoes are even more widely popular today, particularly among environmentally conscious consumers. A number of the company's lines are constructed out of canvas, organic cotton, or even hemp, and the soles are made from recycled rubber. Converse has become a top seller in the "eco-friendly" selection of online shoe retailer Zappos.

Nike and Converse have pretty divergent images when it comes to social responsibility. Yet they are now part of the same company—Nike purchased Converse after the latter went bankrupt in 2001. By keeping the branding separate, Nike is extending itself into markets that the parent brand would not be able to reach. Fashion house Armani made a similar move, with different motivations, when it created separate brands for different demographic markets: Giorgio Armani for the couture line, Armani Exchange for everyday fashion, XO for young shoppers.

Then there is Google, which has extended its brand from search (Google.com), to video (YouTube), to operating systems (Android), to devices (Droid and Google TV). All of these moves are connected by information, meaning they are all arguably part of Google's core business of making information available and analyzable. But they show how a brand can potentially take a core expertise and make it applicable to different platforms and media.

Package Innovation Pitfalls

Package innovation is possibly the most straightforward of the three revenue innovation approaches. What company doesn't have a backlog of delayed or discarded marketing or packaging ideas? Conceptually, innovating around product packaging seems an obvious and lucrative approach to take. Yet, of the three, package innovation can be the most difficult to accomplish.

There are a few reasons for this, the most relevant of which is timing. More often than not, companies that develop value integration or extensions are responding to a trend once it is already under way. If you don't understand the behaviors that are driving the trend, you won't be able to segment properly, and your efforts are likely to disappear into the noise of a "hot" market. By the time you get something on the market, the audience has already moved on. You'll certainly never get ahead of the curve where the most revenue and profit opportunity lives.

That need for rapid response, coupled with a general difficulty of knowing what people will buy, makes package innovation inherently risky, just like the introduction of any new product. These realities should make componentization and mash-ups attractive options, since they involve taking products that are already designed and repurposing them for new uses.

Another challenge of package innovation is that the innovations often require companies to develop a new set of skills or to compete in unfamiliar markets. Particularly in the case of value integration or extensions, the new packages and value propositions may not fit well with the company culture. Few product companies have found it easy to move successfully into services. The sales force is accustomed to pushing transactions over relationships, and compensation structures are rarely structured to adequately reward long-term customer retention. Perhaps that is why Best Buy's success in services was achieved through an acquisition. Note as well that the company kept the Geek Squad brand.

Componentization businesses are not immune to operational challenges. The part may be priced less than the whole, requiring you to develop a capacity for processing micropayments or evolve a culture comfortable with pushing many low-price transactions over few high-value sales.

A third challenge around package innovation relates particularly to componentized or mash-up products and the issues of rights management. Record labels were late to embrace mash-ups because of the challenges of revenue allocation. Some commercial songs already borrow a baseline from here or a hook from there. Couple that with the multiple tracks layered in a mash-up, and it can get very difficult to get permissions and allocate revenues—so difficult that the revenue opportunity is eroded and the labels no longer gain value.

Yet, there is a subset of customers who want to exercise their own creativity and control, and they are going to find ways to cut and remix music, video, game snippets, and information with or without the cooperation of content owners. So why not try to monetize it? Some services are evolving to make it easier to compensate content owners. Google's Content ID makes it more likely that the component used will come with its owner-identifying ID. These work-arounds will likely get better over time and turn digital rights issues into a manageable challenge.

Package Innovation Lessons

The examples of what has already happened in package innovation, and what seems likely to come, offer a few lessons for companies as they brainstorm where their products might go. The first is to jump on trends early. You might not need to be the first to identify them, but you do need to be early to respond. Digital product life cycles are short—months, not years. As we are seeing with ringtones, it took less than ten years between when the market took off and when it began its retreat.

The second lesson is to match early response with accurate assessment of the behavioral segments so you can develop appropriate pricing models for the new packages and the value perceived in different segments. Young consumers were willing to spend more than $2.00 to buy ringtones, when logic might have said that twenty seconds of song should have had a price of $0.50 or less. Perhaps the success in this case comes from audacity—sellers set the price at $2.00, and customers set their expectations around that.

The third lesson is to get comfortable with greater risk and uncertainty. Splitting products into their component parts may cause consumers to use those components in ways you had never intended. You may no longer see your product presented in favorable ways.

Take Nike's experience with shoe componentization. In 2000 the company created a Web service that allowed consumers to create their own shoe by matching chosen parts. Nike wanted to give consumers an opportunity to personalize their shoes. Most customers used the service benignly—to match silver insteps with hot pink soles, for example. But MIT student Jonah Peretti tried to customize his Nike sneakers with "Sweatshop" stitched into the instep, sparking a private exchange that went public and reactivated public criticism of the shoe company.[12] Such creative expression is admittedly less than great for the brand, but it does not negate the value of capitalizing on the revenue potential of letting customers work with the parts instead of the whole. The fact is that activists and others will componentize your product for their purposes anyway—you may as well benefit from componentization.[13]

A corollary point, and the fourth lesson, is to get used to ambiguity surrounding what your product really is and who your competitors are. Ten years ago, Best Buy would have seen its prime competition coming from other consumer electronics retailers, such as Circuit City, CompUSA, and even Walmart. Today, it fights competition from AT&T for handheld device sales and from Time Warner Cable for DVR functionality. In 2010 it's again shifting its position by offering Best Buy–branded laptops.

Relative value continues to shift in the digital space, depending on the product and the market. The way to combat price erosion or value shifts is to become more flexible. Music labels used to see products only as physical recordings. Now products are individual songs, and even cuts from concert and merchandise revenue. By not thinking too myopically about what defines a product or space, companies can find more opportunities to expand their revenue-generating reach.

Of course, some opportunities may be best addressed through partnerships, or even acquisitions. Thus the fifth lesson is to embrace collaboration. Best Buy saw an opportunity to develop a services capability without developing those skills in-house. Disney also saw a chance to leverage Apple's retail expertise for its own purposes. In the current environment, in which digitization is creating all sorts of convergence of content, devices, and services, linkages between companies that can provide different pieces of the puzzle are even more critical. This is not to say that those linkages are easily made. "Not created here" thinking is alive and well in corporations—and it is very dangerous in the digital space. Knowing where your expertise lies and where you need help can allow for faster, more effective package innovation.

Getting Started

Table 4-1 provides a summary of package innovation. So what are some of the early questions you can ask in pursuit of package innovation? Package innovation requires an expansive view of what your products or product parts might be and where they could add value. Here are some questions to ask.

Strategy

- How are consumers using your product? Is it as you intended?

- What industry do you play in now? Where might you like to play in three or five years?

- What partnerships do you have in place, or could you create, to enable package innovation and integration across content, hardware, software, and services?

Infrastructure

- Do you have the analytics in place to identify trends in behavior and usage of products?

- Does your infrastructure enable you to componentize, mash up, integrate, or extend your products flexibly?

TABLE 4-1

Package innovation in brief

Model	Traditional mode	Innovation	Digital-era-example
Componentization	Buyers assemble product from predefined parts, as with software "suites"	Split product or in-house resources into component parts and monetize in a different form for a different customer or use: recombine into mash-ups	• Ringtones • Video game "creators" • Amazon "1-Click" • Vessel Tracker
Value integration	Add services within product structures, i.e, as a lease on capital equipment or service charge on a software license	Add up- or downstream opportunities within the same value chain, whether from product to services or service-to-service plays	• Interface Carpet Leasing • Creative or analytic services on ad sales • Nespresso
Value extension	Extend the same brand into a parallel sector, common with "celebrity" brands like Martha Stewart	Extend into parallel sectors with a brand geared toward the demands and purchase behaviors of the segment	• Tyra Banks • Nike and Converse

Operations

• Can your organization evolve to add services within a product culture, or vice versa?

• What partnerships would you need to deliver a seamless experience across the value chain?

CONCLUSION

Launching Innovation

I n April 2009 an unusual contraption appeared in a corner of a popular bookstore in London. The machine, dubbed the Espresso Book Machine, literally makes books. Part copy machine, part digital printer, part Gutenberg press, the Espresso allows bookstore customers to print and bind any one of millions of titles on demand in minutes.

Looking for an obscure novel you remember from twenty years ago? The Espresso delivers. The machine won't have the latest best seller—those are already stocked on the shelves. The Espresso's sweet spot is book publishing's long tail, where rare, out-of-print, esoteric, or low-demand titles find new life.

The machine's creator, On Demand Books (ODB), sells its machine for roughly $100,000. The major takers to date have been university stores, iconic booksellers, and libraries. There is a certain symbolic relevance to seeing a machine that can get any book in the Bibliotheca Alexandrina in Alexandria, Egypt, for example, or the New York Public Library. The Espresso is also designed for the self-publishing industry: anyone with a USB drive can upload, print, and bind a few copies of their master's thesis, small-business sales pitch, annual report, baby journal, or even their "great American novel," within minutes.[1] A sales and distribution partnership with Xerox may move the device even further beyond the thirty or so bookstore and library installations it already has.

Revenue Innovation: Doing More with What You Have

The Espresso Book Machine is an interesting application for our age because it is so unlikely. In an era when the biggest news in publishing is the battle between Apple and Amazon for control of the e-book ecosystem, a machine that allows readers to get physical versions of rare books seems hopelessly anachronistic. And yet millions of readers still buy physical books. For them, and for the booksellers they buy from, the Espresso looks like an alternative innovation to Amazon that still breaks through the limitations of shelf space. So what is the best way to reach those reading millions? What behaviors do they exhibit? What pricing, payer, or package models will best appeal to them?

These questions about the go-to-market strategy for an innovation like the Espresso Book Machine are familiar to many of you working in other media and nonmedia industries. Namely, you know that growth opportunities depend on innovation, but technology change happens unevenly across consumer segments, and the installed base is often lucrative and resistant to change. Successful innovation means capturing opportunity at the "right" rate in the right venues to gain maximum profitability from both the existing revenue streams and the future ones.

I mentioned in the introduction that one of the advantages of revenue innovation over other business model innovation approaches is that it allows you to identify new revenue streams from existing assets, including products, customers and customer relationships, skill sets, brands, research data, and in-house knowledge. There are lots of options and opportunities for revenue innovation around alternative payer, packaging, and pricing strategies, but where should you start? Is it best to focus on just one innovation path or all three at once? Are there approaches that make more sense in certain industries or among certain customer segments?

There are some pointers to give you direction as you start looking at revenue innovation—specifically, a four-step process for innovating new revenue approaches: first, look at the behavioral segments you serve now and the ones you would like to serve in the future; second, use the three-model framework of pricing, payer, and package innovation to evaluate what approaches are common in your industry and which might offer opportunities for revenue innovation; third, experiment; fourth, repeat.

What are some current digital consumer attitudes that may affect your success? Where are revenue innovations happening and why? Where will companies go from here? How are innovations crossing and comingling? What do the more successful approaches have in common? I'll try to answer some of these questions here.

There's also the question of getting innovation done. No company sets out to become staid, but inertia is one of the strongest forces in the universe, making innovation difficult to execute even when bankruptcy and oblivion are real alternatives. While this book isn't about the process of innovation, I'll offer some brief musings on the innovation approaches I've seen and how to get innovation done with the greatest chance of success.

Innovation and Consumer Segments

When I work with clients to develop revenue strategies, I advise that they look first at the customer and behavioral segments they currently serve and the ones they want to serve in the future, to identify opportunities to offer value up and down the value chain. Your existing customers, for better or for worse, will drive how you pursue new revenue streams.

While your existing customers and your existing revenue stream are in the driver's seat, that doesn't mean you should stick to your current approach to segmenting and targeting those customers. Remember that the goal is to view consumers not only through their demographic or psychographic characteristics but through the lens of their behaviors: What product volumes do they consume? How do they use the product and how often? How do they interact with or alter the product through use and through the addition of information to supplement their experience?

Conclusion

This is not a one-and-done exercise. You will need to be constantly monitoring the flow of data to see how behaviors are changing. Otherwise, you risk launching innovations that miss their mark because the mark has moved. The problem is analogous to what Clayton Christensen lays out in his canonical books, *The Innovator's Dilemma* and *The Innovator's Solution*.[2] The same once successful behaviors and approaches become blinders when markets change, just as outdated ideas of who your customers are cause blunders when their behaviors and attitudes shift.

Consider the perception of social media sites like Facebook and Twitter as digital playgrounds for the Kool Kids. Corporate social media campaigns that utilize these sites aim to connect with younger demographics. Yet the largest group of Facebook users is women between the ages of thirty-five and fifty-four, and users over fifty-five make up more than 10 percent of the audience.[3] Kool Kids also use Twitter at a far lower rate than they use other social media and far less frequently than Gadgetiers, despite the fact that the platform evolved out of the quintessential Kool Kid behavior of texting.

Surprised? Lots of people I talk to are, but that's because they've locked into a view of Kool Kids that doesn't change. In reality, the first generation of Kids is already aging into Gadgetiers and Massive Passives. Massive Passive behaviors are shifting too. Nearly 70 percent of Americans use the Internet as one of their primary sources of news, according to a recent Pew study.[4] More than 40 percent of adults use a phone to check the Internet, use e-mail, and instant-message. If your grandmother is still alive, she just might be reading e-mail on her iPhone. YouTube has introduced its Leanback product specifically for people on the cusp of being Massive Passive. In other words, Massive Passives are just about at the point where they are consuming television on their computers.

Attitudes within your consumer base about how "free" certain types of value should be may also be considered at the customer evaluation stage of the innovation process. Don't take anything for granted. IBM's 2010 Digital Consumer Survey shows that willingness to pay doesn't at all fall into the neat segment categories you might expect.[5] Gadgetiers are more likely than members of other segments to express willingness to pay, but Massive Passives are the least likely to want to pay at all— they did, after all, grow up with free-to-air radio and television. Curiously, a greater proportion of Kool Kids are willing to pay directly for content than Massive Passives, probably because they are more accustomed to the pay-per-view model (even if they often find ways around it).

Keep in mind that this data doesn't show the full picture, since self-reported behaviors are notoriously false. When consumers say they won't pay for content, it means they don't want to, not that they won't. You can influence behavior by making something easy to do. Perhaps only 20 percent of consumers are willing to pay for online content because some fraction of the rest finds existing payment methods cumbersome. Improve online payment options, and more consumers may willingly open their (digital) wallets.

The lessons from media on looking to the customer base for opportunities lean largely toward what *not* to do at this first stage of the innovation process. In short, don't just look at what your consumer segments are doing now but what they *want* to be doing, or will be doing, in the future. Don't just look at where you operate in your value chain but where value might be shifting and what you would have to do to play there as well.

Media's big names in many cases put far more resources into halting revenue loss from their existing customers based on existing behaviors than in innovating new revenue sources. As a result, the digital initiatives of most traditional media companies are overtly not revenue innovations. Porting existing content and revenue models onto a different platform is not an innovation. Nonetheless, the approach is popular among incumbents, as evidenced by Hulu, the *New York Times*, Comcast's proposed TV Everywhere, and many other media efforts. To its credit, Hulu is certainly a success story in amassing audience. But the primary offering of the site is exactly the same product in exactly the same spot on the value chain with the same payers. Hulu's owners have largely prevented it from experimenting with ways to really appeal to Kool Kids and Gadgetiers. Even Hulu's new subscription model is a weak attempt at pricing innovation, given the seemingly random mix of free and pay content and the confusion around what the subscription includes.

In contrast, most of the real innovations in media have come from new entrants or parallel initiatives that, if successful over the long term, will blow up traditional economic models: Redbox in film rental, Spotify in music, Amazon's Kindle in e-books, Google TV in television, and Craigslist in newspaper classifieds.

It is not hard to see why those who work for incumbent firms have so much trouble thinking outside existing views of the customer and existing monetization models: they have established partnerships and an installed base of customers they want to keep happy. Likewise, there is the pervasive fear that any move to digital services won't earn because users won't move beyond free. The data from the 2010 Digital Consumer Survey outlined above shows how both true and false that statement can be.

The most important takeaway lesson here is about the continually changing dynamics that happen when you look at the customer through the lens of what they are really doing—not what they may do based on their age, gender, political views, and so on. Your segmentation will evolve with customers and markets, and you will need to adjust as they do.

Pricing, Payer, Package: Opportunities by Industry

Whether consumer attitudes toward paying for content and ad-driven models have come about because of what they are used to seeing from providers or because of innate preference, the natural conclusion we can draw from those numbers is that media companies have adopted advertising, sponsorship, and product placement more often than pay models in the digital sphere—and in fact that is the case. Experiments in pricing and package innovation have taken minority positions, but there have still been some significant success stories, as we have seen in the market for ringtones and for iPhone apps.

For the most part, revenue innovations have come as individual, siloed efforts. Firms try out an ad model and see how it goes. Or they try a package innovation and give it some time to take hold. To date there has not been much, if any, mixing of revenue innovation approaches or structuring of new revenue models for specific user segments. That siloed approach is temporary. As you become more comfortable with individual revenue innovations, you will see the opportunities to add parallel or complementary efforts. In 2010, we have already seen a rapid increase in pricing innovations. Package innovation, by far the most difficult of the three, will increase but will remain the minority approach.

The Current State of Payer Innovation

Information companies largely turned first to advertising as a digital revenue model. Print media has mostly abandoned subscriptions and relied on ads in the digital realm. The exceptions—the *Financial Times,* the *Wall Street Journal,* the *Economist,* and soon the *New York Times*—are easier to exhaust than the rules. Sixty-two percent of total media revenues in the digital sphere in 2009 came from advertising, compared with 40 percent from advertising for analog products.

Only a fraction of this ad revenue can be counted as true payer innovation in the sense that it fulfills the definition I laid out in the third chapter. To recap, for an advertising or sponsorship model to be a payer innovation, it must (1) be applied to an industry where advertising or sponsorship has no tradition; (2) be applied in more targeted and integrated ways; and/or (3) be applied in a new or nascent industry. Note from the examples in chapter 3 that most of the examples of innovation come less from the traditional leaders in media and more from information sectors—software, search, and telecom.

Conclusion

The disproportionate dominance of payer innovation today among the three revenue innovation approaches is temporary, and it will remain a side note outside of information-focused industries. Walmart's use of advertising to supplement retail revenues will continue to be an unusual application. IBM projections show that the percentage of revenues provided by traditional advertising will decline by 4 percent to 58 percent of the whole by 2013, with a continued slow downward trend expected over time. That doesn't mean that advertising itself will decrease. Rather, in a growing digital market, traditional advertising will account for a smaller piece of the pie. The ad models that survive will be marked by more targeting and relevance and more innovation in nontraditional markets. They will have to, since consumers will come to expect ad relevance, and the technology for targeted marketing will only improve. As time goes on, pricing and package innovations will become more important, and they will more frequently coexist with payer models.

The Rise of Pricing

Innovations in pricing became more common in 2010 and will become more popular still. To date, many of the existing experiments in payer innovation and pricing innovation have been siloed—one innovation per company—but that will change as companies experiment more with alternative pricing. In many cases, pricing innovations will complement, not replace, extant payer models: newspapers and television will likely keep dual revenue lines of advertising and subscriptions or metered pricing. That's the approach planned by the *New York Times* and the *Times* of London, as well as by Hulu.

Conclusion

Digital television, music, consumer technology, and financial services will support payer and pricing innovations in tiered pricing models or other variable pricing approaches. Note that what these industries have in common is a mass-market consumer base, extreme variation in the willingness to pay of the target customer, and significant competition. Other industries with like characteristics can look to pricing innovations in these sectors for lessons.

Many industries have historically been resistant to experiments in pricing, so innovation in this area is long overdue. Even as I write this, media firms whose digital models have relied on ads are announcing or implementing pricing innovation: venerable but struggling news organizations like the *New York Times*, *Time* magazine, and the *Times* of London will all have paywalls by 2011. Hulu began its subscription service in 2010, and Spotify all but shut off new subscriptions for its ad-supported service; new members can start listening right away only for a fee.

Outside of media, pricing innovation will be a preferred revenue innovation approach in health care and utilities. In the pricing chapter, I gave examples of health-care providers offering primary care membership services for the poor, or pharmaceutical companies experimenting with "pay-for-performance" approaches. As government pressure to contain health-care costs increases around the world, more providers will look for creative ways to comply with government mandates, improve care, and find new revenue streams. Among electric utilities, smart meter technology is giving both consumers and utilities more accurate information on peak times and downtimes, which allows the providers to offer advantageous pricing for consumers willing to adjust their consumption.

Package Innovation Along the Value Chain

Package innovation is the most difficult of the three innovation approaches, and as a result it will be the least popular revenue innovation approach, with half as many package innovations pursued as pricing innovation in the coming years. Those of you operating in highly competitive markets and serving customer segments that have expressed willingness to pay more for an integrated experience may find opportunities to repackage your product.

The current battle for dominance between Amazon and Apple offers an example of a package innovation battle that is already under way. Advertising has been the traditional cross-subsidy model for media, but increasingly for companies like Amazon and Apple, expensive devices are cross-subsidizing the content. But as devices like the iPad and its soon-to-be many competitors enter the market, there will be pressure on everyone's margins. Already Amazon has cut the Kindle's price by roughly 40 percent in the last year. As the television competes with the PC, which competes with the handheld, which competes with the tablet, companies are lining up to provide the content, pitting Walmart against Comcast, and Google against Hewlett-Packard. Meanwhile, there's going to continue to be a flood of new entrants, like Sezmi, ZillionTV, and Digiboo, competing with each other and with the established players. In many cases there will be competing models of cross-subsidization, which will make predicting winners and losers or figuring out the appropriate competitive response all the more challenging.

Although package innovations will be less common overall than either pricing or payer innovations, they will dominate certain industries. For example, B2B software in the past ten years has largely focused on package innovations, whether by bundling or componentizing functionality, or by packaging software as a service (SaaS) so that the vendor manages the software platform and setup, the server and network management, user keys, and other elements of the total cost of ownership. Financial services has also tried to do more to integrate complementary products, such as deposits and investments, or homeowner's insurance with a mortgage loan.

You might rightly look at the opportunities and determine that package innovation is not for your company. Be aware, nonetheless, how a package innovation outside of your industry could bring new competition. Telecom's package innovations brought life to mobile payments, for instance, allowing consumers and merchants in Kenya and the Philippines, among other places, to bypass banks for money movement; Microsoft added more value to Sync than Ford; and Amazon knocked Sony out of presumed dominance in e-book readers. In package innovation, the components outside your industry may just be the ones that everyone suddenly needs.

For some industries, package innovation will only be possible after they have pursued payer or pricing innovations. This is partly a function of ease—pricing and payer innovations are just easier to do. Mostly, however, the evolution is a function of market readiness. Pricing often has to come first so you can gather necessary information about the required consumer behaviors and willingness to pay that will allow you to do package innovation well.

Utilities, for example, are experimenting with pricing innovation because smart meter technology is only now allowing them to move from the pay-as-you-go models that so long dominated. Both the utilities and the consumers are entering an adjustment period during which they learn to use and react to new information. The futuristic view of the industry in which all household appliances are linked under one system is still far off and can only happen once consumers and utilities alike learn to react to smart information. The reaction of some early users of smart meters in California was to sue the utilities because they simply didn't believe what the meters were telling them.

Health care may see a similar multistep transition from pricing innovation to package innovation in the United States, as government pressures to contain costs, coupled with electronic medical records initiatives, drive price changes and better information. Table C-1 summarizes some of the factors that will make different types of revenue innovation more appealing in certain industries.

Experiments in Innovation

Innovation is never a straight path, nor will successes ever outnumber failed experiments—Abbie Griffin's assertion that 85 percent of new products fail has only proved more true over time.[6] There is no fixed combination that all companies will adopt, either by industry or by target customer segment. The

Conclusion

TABLE C-1

Cross-industry revenue innovation approaches

	Payer	Pricing	Package
Value proposition	• Scale • Ability to aggregate desirable niche audiences	• Unique content • Preferential access • Improved alliance of payment and consumption	• Superior experience (convenience, mobility, integration, functionality, ease of use)
Degree of competition and industry structure	• High • Fragmented	• High	• Moderate
Industries	• Media • Event management/ promotion • Telecommunications • Consumer technology • Consumer packaged goods • Retail	• Media • Information and research • Health care • Utilities • Retail	• Hardware and device manufacturing • Retail • Information aggregation • Software • Financial services

only way to find an ideal mix, if temporarily, is to experiment with different models for different segments, and be willing to rapidly shift to new experiments as you learn and as segments, technology, and competitors change—all faster than you expect.

The Espresso Book Machine offers a valuable thought exercise in thinking through ways to take what you know about your assets and your consumer base to define productive revenue innovation experiments.

The Espresso can print any one of half a million titles on demand, a cool option for the world's bibliophiles—all twelve of them. With demand for physical books falling steadily, a $100,000 device that custom manufactures physical books does not seem to have much of a market over the long term. The access it offers to rare or out-of-print titles, for instance, is not for the Gadgetier, who is now happily reading from a Kindle, iPhone, iPad, or Sony eReader. Nor is it for the Kool Kids—they've never been readers of print books. Avid Massive Passive readers who still want books on paper and tire of always needing to wait for an out-of-stock or unusual title are the right segment for the on-demand book-printing services offered by the Espresso. At that price, a book-seller would have to sell 12,500 books at $8 a copy before it started turning a profit, not including maintenance costs and upgrades. Do readers have enough interest in delving into the long tail to make it worth it? And given that the market is shrinking, are there other ways beyond traditional unit book sales and traditional readers to monetize the machine?

There may be. Consider universities and booksellers: for them, access to millions of rare inventory items, coupled with on-demand printing capability, offers an opportunity in revenue innovation. On-demand printing is package innovation at its finest, and there is no reason to price the output strictly by units. Prices could vary depending on the popularity of the title, its rarity, the proportion of text to image, and so on. Heavy users could be enticed to buy a prepaid subscription that allows them to print a certain number of books. Payer innovation is not out of the question either. The New York Public Library allowed patrons to print titles free of charge, effectively adopting a government subsidy model.

Nor are traditional universities and booksellers the only channels through which the Espresso can reach readers. The commercial possibilities seem even greater for business consumers with custom runs of annual reports, white papers, and research results. It was the World Bank, after all, that ran the first beta installation of the machine and allowed custom runs of the thousands of World Bank reports and publications produced each year.

Then there are the self-publishing opportunities that On Demand Books offers through a partnership with Lightning Source. Thousands of masters' theses, annual family updates slipped into the holiday cards, small-business marketing collateral, and that novel you finally finished and just wanted to see in print could build incremental revenue for the company. A distribution deal that On Demand Books now has with Xerox opens the possibility that the Espresso Book Machine may become common in retail office supply stores like FedEx Office and Staples as a self-serve option for small businesses to create short runs of custom documents.

I don't know that On Demand Books is considering any of these options. Indeed, from the perspective of On Demand Books, the Espresso Book Machine is probably not a revenue innovation at all, but an industry innovation that is moving book publishing away from centralized printing and distribution to decentralized printing that effectively makes distribution requirements disappear. The company calls it an "ATM for books," an unfortunate excess of metaphor for a machine named the Espresso. But just thinking about what the company might pursue shows how innovation approaches could vary and overlap. The best innovation at any given time may be dictated by what customers it serves, where it resides in the value chain, and the current dynamics of the industry.

The Innovation Organization

So you've identified the consumer segments you serve and the ones you want to serve in the future; you've evaluated where you operate in the value chain and where the value may go. Maybe you even have some ideas for payer, pricing, or package innovations ideal for your company. How do you give those innovations the greatest opportunity for survival?

There is a great deal of change management literature out there that talks about the ways to prepare and organize for innovation. It is beyond the scope of this book to either rehash or compete with it. The dot-com era produced plenty of case studies on the difficulty of building digital businesses within existing organizations, and I do not think that the dynamics have particularly changed since then. Nonetheless, companies still seem to make the same mistakes and face the same challenges as their peers over and over, so it is worth mentioning four issues that can help or hinder innovation: the organization, the talent, the complexity, and the metrics.

First, the organization. Many companies that put a premium on new innovation tackle it by creating a separate entity responsible for new business creation. The reasons for this are as old as the Greek gods: like Kronos, the powerful tend to eat their young. In media, this means that traditional businesses tend to kill the new. Salespeople may give the digital product away as a sweetener, or employees hoard resources and handicap new efforts. Creating a separate organization shields the new initiative and gives it a chance to grow. But such separation also prevents cross-platform integration and consistency and creates us-versus-them antagonism that stymies collaboration and frustrates customers. Creating a separate entity for innovation also sends a message to the core company that innovation is something that happens *over there* and doesn't need to be part of everyone's job.

Consider as well the talent needed to make innovation happen. Plenty of companies don't have the right skills in the right places necessary to innovate. A company that has focused on unit sales might lack personnel in accounting who can create a subscription pricing structure; splitting your product into parts may move you from a low-volume, high-profit business to a high-volume, low-profit system that your customer relationship management (CRM), inventory management, and other logistics and operational systems cannot handle. This challenge can go all the way down to the level of corporate culture: you may see a chance to offer services as an additional revenue source within your product-focused business, but your salespeople were hired because of their skills in closing unit-focused deals. You are going to have to retrain them, and not all of them are going to be enthusiastic. Don't take the questions at the end of each of the previous chapters lightly. Far too many promising innovation projects fail because the company doesn't recognize the skills gap until it is too late.

Third, consider simplicity when developing new programs. One of the reasons why Apple iTunes has so successfully dominated the online music business is that the online store and the device are designed with such plug-and-play simplicity. So many companies hinder their own efforts by making a program too difficult to decipher—the modern consumer doesn't have a lot of time or patience to figure things out, not when there are easier alternatives available. Hulu, I would venture, is falling into that trap with a first pass at a subscription program that is just as opaque as analog cable subscriptions. Make something easy to do, and you might find less resistance from your target customers.

Last, consider your criteria for innovation success. What does the new business have to achieve to be considered successful? What elements are you including in that evaluation? Is success measured in audience accrual or in revenue or in profits, or in growth rates of any of the above? Do the costs for the new business include its portion of costs shared with the traditional business, or are those costs off-loaded? In media, many digital businesses went live with the executive expectation that they meet and exceed the value of the traditional product. Is that approach fair? How long do you give a new business before you call it a success or a failure? If Hulu had charged in the beginning, would anyone have used it? Now that the site has an audience and is "breaking even," the traditional side of the business is complaining that the site pays nothing for its content—those costs are all loaded onto the traditional revenue models. Consider not just the "fair" way to account for costs, but the useful way to account for costs so that you can make good business decisions about future investments in alternative revenue models.

The most important thing is to actively make these decisions up front rather than after the fact. These choices will inevitably play a major role in whether any innovation is considered successful or not—but have nothing to do with the quality or utility of the innovation itself. I've seen far too many promising innovations killed by the use of default accounting, and far too many projects green-lighted that were always going to be in the red because costs weren't properly considered. In summary, finance has to be part of your revenue innovation team.

A Final Warning from the Media Industry

There have been plenty of examples of missteps in the digital era on the part of the media industry. It's easy now to see those mistakes, laugh and enjoy a bit of schadenfreude, and wonder how "they" could have been so dumb.

Let me assure you that the executives who made the choices that now look so shortsighted were by no means dumb. They did not lack the genes for self-preservation. No one I've met was indifferent to future revenue streams. They believed the decisions they were making were the right ones for their businesses. In all of the most important ways, they are just like you.

Do not think that you and your colleagues won't make some of the same mistakes as the media industry has. Do not think that you are invulnerable to being blindsided by technology change, market change, or new competitors. Do not think that it will not be difficult to innovate your revenue model as rapidly and as thoroughly as you need to. Do not think that you have "plenty of time" to work things out.

Those are exactly the same mistakes that media made. Too many of the executives thought they had more time, thought they had a good read of the market, thought they could wait for "better" ideas and options to come along. They neglected opportunities, failed to invest in revenue innovation, stuck to their segmentations, pricing, payers, and packaging not because they were dumb or blind but because they were normal.

The easy path, the normal path, is to find all the reasons not to innovate your revenue models rather than seizing opportunities for revenue innovation. Don't be normal. Don't take the easy way out. There are no second chances, and the clock is ticking.

NOTES

Introduction

1. Growth (and loss) statistics are taken from the *Pricewaterhouse-Coopers Global Entertainment and Media Outlook: 2010–2014.*

2. Numbers on the video rental market are from NPD Group, a market research firm. Some useful reporting on the success of the *Financial Times'* digital strategies is available at the paidcontent.org site in the article, "Financial Times Content/Revs to Overtake Print Ad Revs This Year," January 4, 2010: http://paidcontent.org/article/419-ft-exceeded-2009-targets-as-owner-pearson-raises-forecast/; and http://paidcontent.co.uk/article/419-financial-times-contentcharging-revs-to-overtake-print-ad-revs-this-yea/.

3. In the past eighteen months, several books dedicated to business model innovation have been published. They include John Mullins and Randy Komisar, *Getting to Plan B: Breaking Through to a Better Business Model* (Boston: Harvard Business Press, 2009); Mark W. Johnson, *Seizing the White Space: Business Model Innovation for Growth and Renewal* (Boston: Harvard Business Press, 2010); and Alexander Osterwalder and Yves Pigneur, *Business Model Generation: A Handbook for Visionaries, Game Changers, and Challengers* (Hoboken, NJ: Wiley, 2010).

4. Jim Collins, *How the Mighty Fall: And Why Some Companies Never Give In* (New York: HarperCollins, 2009).

5. Jim Adams, Edgar Mounib, and Amnon Shabo, *IT-Enabled Personalized Healthcare: Improving the Science of Health Promotion and Care Delivery,* IBM Global Business Services Executive Report, April 2010.

6. The first IBM CEO study was conducted in 2004 and has been repeated every two years since then, each time with a larger pool of interviewees. The results from the 2006 study of 765 global CEOs and

senior executives were used to quantify that companies engaging in business model innovation had better financial results than their peers. Questions about what constituted *business model innovation* in the eyes of the CEOs were pursued in later years, which allowed us to iteratively expand the pool of research and information. The most recent CEO study, conducted in 2010, had a sample size of more than one thousand respondents. The 2010 CEO study is available at http://www. 935.ibm.com/services/us/ceo/ceostudy2010/index.html.

7. Remarks from Tim Brown's keynote speech at the Global Philanthropy Forum 2010, Redwood City, CA, April 18–21.

8. George S. Day and Paul J. H. Schoemaker, *Peripheral Vision: Detecting the Weak Signals That Will Make or Break Your Company* (Boston: Harvard Business School Press, 2006).

Chapter 1

1. Market share numbers according to NPD Group, a market research company.

2. See the following *New York Times* piece on the threat Redbox poses to the movie studios; article sites market research numbers from NPD Group: Brooks Barnes, "Movie Studios See a Threat in Growth of Redbox," *New York Times*, September 6, 2009, http://www.nytimes.com/2009/09/07/business/media/07redbox.html?_r=1.

3. Academics Ronald Frank, William Massey, and Yolan Wind defined the idea of segmentation basis in the 1970s. Bases are characteristics or variables that define a consumer and perhaps influence his or her purchasing behavior. Bases can be observable or unobservable. Observable bases, for example, include demographics, geographic location, socioeconomic status, and life stage. Unobservable bases include psychographic information, values, personality, and lifestyle.

4. There has been an ongoing debate in segmentation circles as to whether a consumer's demographic profile is in fact a useful tool for predicting behaviors around certain purchases or brands. A 1978 article by Yolan Wind mentions the fact that a call for papers produced no articles that dealt with the results from segmentation approaches. Likewise, the first chapter in the second edition of *Market Segmentation: Conceptual and Methodological Considerations* (The Netherlands: Kluwer Academic Publishers, 2000), written by Michel Wedel and Wagner A. Kamakura, mentions that rigorous research has found demographic segmentation to provide only minimal (and not statistically significant) predictors of behavior.

5. Statistics derived from historical viewing data. http://www.museum.tv/eotvsection.php?entrycode=primetime.

6. Management consulting firm Cap Gemini published a study in October 2009 on the role of the Internet in car purchases, http://www.us.capgemini.com/industries/ind_pressrelease.asp?IndID=16&ID=774.

7. Dionne Searcey and Kate Linebaugh, "Toyota Woes Put Focus on Black Box," *Wall Street Journal*, February 14, 2010, http://online.wsj.com/article/SB10001424052748703562404575067680423734178.html.

8. Moore's categories were originally codified by Stanford professor Everett M. Rogers in his book *Diffusion of Innovations* (New York: Free Press, 1962). Rogers's book offers a discussion on the rate at which consumers adopt new products. Moore then extended the model to talk about adoption of technology innovations: Geoffey Moore, *Crossing the Chasm: Marketing and Selling High-Tech Products to Mainstream Customers* (New York: Harper Business Press, 1991).

9. From the 2010 IBM Global CEO study, "Capitalizing on Complexity," available at http://ibm.com/ceostudy.

10. See Brian Stelter, "On the Web, a Wave of Support for Conan O'Brien," *New York Times* Mediadecoder blog, January 12, 2010, http://mediadecoder.blogs.nytimes.com/2010/01/12/on-the-web-a-wave-of-support-for-conan-obrien/; and Bill Carter, "O'Brien Undone by his Media Hopping Fans," *New York Times*, January 25, 2010, http://www.nytimes.com/2010/01/25/business/media/25conan.html.

11. Bill Carter, "'Tonight Show' Audience a Decade Younger," *New York Times*, July 5, 2009, http://www.nytimes.com/2009/07/06/business/media/06late.html?_r=1.

12. Numbers for digital music as a percentage of the music market come from the International Federation of the Phonographic Industry, http://arstechnica.com/media/news/2009/08/global-digital-music-sales-to-overtake-physical-by-2016.ars.

13. *PricewaterhouseCoopers Global Media Outlook: 2009–2013*, June 2009.

14. Ben Shiller and Joel Waldfogel, "Music for a Song: An Empirical Look at Uniform Song Pricing and Its Alternatives," working paper 15390, National Bureau of Economic Research [NBER], Cambridge, MA, 2009.

15. The music labels traditionally earn revenue only from album sales. Concert revenues and other sources belong to the artist.

16. Tad Friend, "Plugged In," *New Yorker*, August 24, 2009, 50.

17. Andrew Klebanow, "A Psychographic Approach to Customer Segmentation," Urbino.net, http://www.urbino.net/articles.cfm?specific Article=A%20Psychographic%20Approach%20to%20Customer %20Segmentation.

18. Daniel McGinn and Steve Friess, "From Harvard to Las Vegas," *Newsweek*, April 18, 2005, http://www.stevefriess.com/archive/newsweek/ lovemanprofile.htm.

19. Details about Tesco's use of information to drive segmented offers are from Cecilie Rohwedder, "No. 1 Retailer in Britain Uses 'Clubcard' to Thwart Wal-Mart," *Wall Street Journal*, June 6, 2006; and George Day and Christine Moorman, *Strategy from the Outside In: How to Profit from Customer Value* (New York: McGraw-Hill, 2010).

20. Andrew Martin, "Sam's Club Personalizes Discounts for Buyers," *New York Times*, May 30, 2010, http://www.nytimes.com/2010/05/ 31/business/31loyalty.html?scp=1&sq=Sam%27s%20Club%20and% 20discount&st=cse.

21. Blockbuster's 34 percent decline in online subscribers was documented in its second-quarter 2009 10-Q: http://www.sec.gov/ Archives/edgar/data/1085734/000119312509175844/d10q.htm; the 36 percent market share held by mail-based video rental is attributed to NPD Group, a market research firm.

22. Brookes Barnes, "Movie Studios See a Threat in Growth of Redbox," *New York Times*, September 7, 2009, http://www.nytimes. com/2009/09/07/business/media/07redbox.html?_r=1&scp=1&sq=Re d%20Box&st=cse.

23. Ibid.

Chapter 2

1. Jenna Wortham, "A Netflix Model for Haute Couture," *New York Times*, November 9, 2009, http://www.nytimes.com/2009/11/09/ technology/09runway.html?scp=1&sq=dresses%20and%20retnal &st=cse.

2. Psychologists Amos Tversky and Daniel Kahneman, the Nobel laureate, first documented the concept of *loss aversion*, which in practice means that people fear losing what they have more than they want what they don't. Subsequent research estimated that for a new good or service to replace an existing one, its perceived value or benefit to the customer must be in excess of two times the value of the possessed good.

3. C. Edwin Baker, *Advertising and a Democratic Press* (Princeton, NJ: Princeton University Press, 1995), 8.

4. Eric Dash, "Mexican Billionaire Invests in Times Company," *New York Times*, January 12, 2009, http://www.nytimes.com/2009/01/20/business/media/20times.html?scp=3&sq=Times%20and%20Real%20estate%20and%20Carlos%20Slim&st=cse.

5. Helena Murphy, "Making Google Pay, the Axel Springer Way," *Editor's Weblog*, December 9, 2009: http://www.editorsweblog.org/newspaper/2009/12/making_google_pay_the_axel_springer_way.php.

6. Robin Wauter, "The *New York Times* Announces Paid Content Plans for 2011," *TechCrunch*, January 20, 2010, http://techcrunch.com/2010/01/20/new-york-times-metered-model-2011/.

7. Constance Hays, "Variable Price Coke Machine Being Tested," *New York Times*, October 28, 1999, http://www.nytimes.com/1999/10/28/business/variable-price-coke-machine-being-tested.html?pagewanted=1.

8. See, for instance, Meilan Liu and Weiwei Huo, "Dynamic Pricing of Perishable Goods in Electronic Markets," *International Journal of Business Strategy* (May 2007); Y. Narahari, C. V. L. Raju, K. Ravikumar, and Sourabh Shah, "Dynamic Pricing Models for Electronic Business." *Sādhanā* 30, part 2 and 3 (2005): 231–256, abstract available at: http://jobfunctions.bnet.com/abstract.aspx?docid=242537&tag=content;col1; V. Jayaraman and Tim Baker, "The Internet as an Enabler of Dynamic Pricing of Goods," *IEEE Transactions on Engineering Management* 50, no. 4 (2003), abstract available at: http://jobfunctions.bnet.com/abstract.aspx?tag=content%3Bcol1&docid=242836&promo=100511; and K. L. Haws and W. O. Bearden, "Dynamic Pricing and Consumer Fairness Perceptions," *Journal of Consumer Research* 33, no. 3 (2006).

9. Randy Komisar and Kent Lineback, *The Monk and the Riddle: The Education of a Silicon Valley Entrepreneur* (Boston: Harvard Business School Press, 2001).

10. Eliot van Buskirk, "Comscore: 2 Out of 5 Downloaders Paid for Radiohead's 'In Rainbows' (Average Price $6)," *Wired*, November 5, 2007, http://www.wired.com/listening_post/2007/11/comscore-2-out/.

11. Brian B. Spear, Margo Heath-Chiozzi, and Jeffrey Huff, "Clinical Application of Pharmacogenetics," *Clinical Trends in Molecular Medicine* 7, no. 5 (2001).

12. Jacob Goldstein, "Pay for Performance for Prescription Drugs, Or Maybe Not," *Wall Street Journal*, April 23, 2009, http://blogs.

wsj.com/health/2009/04/23/pay-for-performance-for-prescription-drugs-or-maybe-not/.

13. A Nielsen study from 2007 quantified the number of channels watched in the average household, as reported by the *New York Daily News*: Richard Huff, "Average Joe See Just 15 Channels," *New York Daily News,* March 20, 2007: http://www.nydailynews.com/entertainment/tv/2007/03/20/2007-03-20_average_joe_sees_just_15_channels-1.html.

14. CelrunTV corporate Web site reporting on HanaroTV's customer acquisition success from August 30, 2007: http://www.celruntv.com/news_view.asp?bco_seq=45.

15. Gary Kim, "Will Mobile Advertising be 1% or 20% of Service Provider Revenue?" *Mobile Marketing and Technology,* May 2010, http://www.mobilemarketingandtechnology.com/tag/cable-advertising/.

16. Cisco Visual Networking Index, June 2009.

17. "Redbox's Vending Machines Are Giving Netflix Competition," the Associated Press, June 2009, http://www.nytimes.com/2009/06/22/business/media/22redbox.html?sq=RedBox&st=cse&adxnnl=1&scp=2&adxnnlx=1257966075-FxUK4i8EabnQwiw3Ej4oZA.

18. Statistics from the trade organization Digital Entertainment Group.

19. Michael Cieply, "Studios Spying on Redbox Kiosks," *New York Times*, November 17, 2009: http://mediadecoder.blogs.nytimes.com/2009/11/17/studios-spying-on-redbox-kiosks/?scp=1&sq=redbox%20and%20studios&st=cse.

20. Dawn C. Chmielewski, "Redbox Reaches Settlement with Universal Studios/Twentieth Century Fox," *LA Times*, April 22, 2010, http://latimesblogs.latimes.com/entertainmentnewsbuzz/2010/04/redbox-reaches-settlement-with-universal-studios-twentieth-century-fox.html.

21. Hannah Elliott, "Pros and Cons of Hourly Car Rentals," *Forbes*, August 19, 2009, http://www.forbes.com/2009/08/19/hourly-car-rentals-lifestyle-vehicles-zipcar-rent-cars.html.

22. Ibid.

23. A case study on Schwab's business model experiments is available at: http://www.docstoc.com/docs/17234565/IT-and-Organizational-Change-in-Digital-Economies-A-Soco.

24. Scott Kirsner, "Reboot: Charles Schwab & Company," *Wired*, November 1999, http://www.wired.com/wired/archive/7.11/schwab_pr.html.

Notes

Chapter 3

1. Statistics about global ad revenues were sourced from the *Price-waterhouseCoopers Global Entertainment and Media Outlook: 2010–2014*.

2. A Finnish company, Blyk at its launch was a mobile virtual network operator (MVNO), which means that it leased airtime from telecommunications carriers such as Orange or O2 in the United Kingdom and then resold those minutes to customers. It owns no infrastructure of its own.

3. James Middleton, "Orange Calls Shots with Mobile Advertising Plan," Telecoms.com, January 26, 2010, http://www.telecoms.com/17593/orange-calls-shots-with-mobile-advertising-plan/.

4. Vicky Woollaston, "Oxford University Bans Spotify," *Web User*, January 17, 2010, http://www.webuser.co.uk/news/top-stories/438937/oxford-university-bans-spotify.

5. IBM 2010 Global Digital Consumer Survey, sample size of 3300.

6. *PricewaterhouseCoopers Global Entertainment and Media Outlook: 2010–2014*.

7. Veronis Suhler Stevenson 2009 Communications Forecast.

8. *MediaPost News*, Online Media Daily, "Report: TV Networks Should Be Afraid—Very Afraid—of Hulu," September 14, 2009, http://www.mediapost.com/publications/?fa=Articles.showArticle&art_aid=113407.

9. Mike Robuck, "Hulu Headed Toward Pay Model, iPad, Xbox," *CED*, June 9, 2010, http://www.cedmagazine.com/News-Hulu-pay-model-iPad-Xbox-060910.aspx.

10. "Wal-Mart Adding Flat-Screen Monitors for In-Store TV Net," *Retail Merchandiser*, November 9, 2004.

11. For a useful synopsis on Blyk and its strategy as of late 2009, see this Yankee Group study: http://about.blyk.com/wp-content/uploads/Yankee-Group-on-Blyk-report1.pdf.

12. Joe Frey, "Progressive's Pay-as-You-Drive Auto Insurance Poised for Wide Rollout," Insure.com, July 18, 2000, http://faculty.msb.edu/homak/HomaHelpSite/WebHelp/Progressive_Autograph_GPS.htm; and Craig Harris, "Customizing Car Insurance," *Canadian Underwriter*, June 2006, http://www.canadianunderwriter.ca/issues/story.aspx?aid=1000204537&type=Print%20Archives

13. Andrew Adam Newman, "A Dream for an Airline and a Hotel Chain," *New York Times*, December 20, 2009, http://www.nytimes.com/2009/12/21/business/media/21adco.html?em.

14. Frederick Balfour and Reena Janna, "Are Olympics Sponsorships Worth It?" *BusinesWeek*, July 31, 2008, http://www.businessweek.com/globalbiz/content/jul2008/gb20080731_125602.htm.

15. Paul Gallagher, "Record Deal Will Keep EMI Rocking," *The Scotsman*, October 3, 2002, http://news.scotsman.com/robbiewilliams/Record-deal-will-keep-EMI.2366213.jp.

16. Lucia Moses, "Magazines Primed to Ride iPad Wave," *Media Week*, April 2, 2010, http://www.adweek.com/aw/content_display/news/e3i0c298f35062573aa973223b4495a62b1.

17. Shira Ovide, "Advertisers Break Out Check Books for iPad Magazine Deals," *Wall Street Journal*, March 25, 2010, http://blogs.wsj.com/digits/2010/03/25/advertisers-break-out-checkbooks-for-ipad-magazine-deals/.

18. Michael Arrington, "Davos Interviews: Ning CEO Gina Bianchini Insists Facebook Isn't a Competitor," *TechCrunch*, February 3, 2010, http://www.techcrunch.com/2010/02/03/davos-interviews-ning-ceo-gina-bianchini-insists-facebook-isnt-a-competitor/.

19. Jason Kincaid, "Ning's Bubble Bursts: No More Free Networks, Cuts 40% of Staff," *TechCrunch*, April 15, 2010, http://techcrunch.com/2010/04/15/nings-bubble-bursts-no-more-free-networks-cuts-40-of-staff/.

20. "So Many Ads, So Few Clicks," *BusinessWeek,* November 12, 2007, http://www.businessweek.com/magazine/content/07_46/b4058053.htm.

21. Jason Kincaid, "Twitter: The World Cup Final Was Our Most Tweeted Event, Ever," *TechCrunch*, July 16, 2010, http://techcrunch.com/2010/07/16/twitter-the-world-cup-final-was-our-most-tweeted-event-ever.

22. A blog post by a Web site monitoring firm on the frequency and effectiveness of tweets: http://royal.pingdom.com/2009/11/13/in-depth-study-of-twitter-how-much-we-tweet-and-when/.

23. Spencer Ante, "Content-Search Deals Make Twitter Profitable," *BusinessWeek*, December 21, 2009, http://www.businessweek.com/technology/content/dec2009/tc20091220_549879.htm.

24. Raghuram Iyengar, Sangman Han, and Sunil Gupta, "Do Friends Influence Friends in a Social Network?" working paper, Harvard Business School, Boston, 2009, http://hbswk.hbs.edu/item/6185.html.

25. Michael Arrington, "Groupon Raises Huge New Round at $1.2 Billion Valuation," *TechCrunch*, April 13, 2010, http://techcrunch.

com/2010/04/13/groupon-raises-huge-new-round-at-1-2-billion-valuation/

26. Statistics were taken from the Gannett 2009 annual report, http://phx.corporate-ir.net/External.File?item=UGFyZW50SU Q9MzcwMjg0fENoaWxkSUQ9MzY3NTYxfFR5cGU9MQ==&t=1.

Chapter 4

1. The percentage of Best Buy's revenue derived from services was taken from the company's 2009 annual report. Service revenue includes warranties.

2. According to Fabrice Grinda, the CEO of Zingy, a New York firm that sells ringtones and cell phone games.

3. The Star Wars Web site announced the game creator in October 2009: http://www.starwars.com/theclonewars/news20091012/index.html.

4. Brooks Barnes, "Disney's Retail Plan Is a Theme Park in Its Stores," *New York Times*, October 13, 2009, http://www.nytimes.com/2009/10/13/business/media/13disney.html.

5. See, for instance, James Fontanella-Khan and Amy Kazmin, "SKS Microfinance Plans to Raise $350m in IPO," *Financial Times*, July 20, 2010, http://www.ft.com/cms/s/0/1879f6e4-9422-11df-a3fe-00144feab49a.html.

6. Publisher's Information Bureau data on advertising sales for the first half of 2009, as compared with sales from the first half of 2008.

7. Stephanie Clifford, "Magazines Now Create and Customize Ads," *New York Times*, September 3, 2009, http://www.nytimes.com/2009/09/04/business/media/04adco.html?scp=3&sq=magazine%20and%20Lexus&st=cse.

8. Google recently won a summary judgment in a court case brought against it by Viacom, which claimed that Google was violating copyright by letting users post professional content. The judge ruled that Google always took the content down when asked, and so had done no wrong. Erick Schonfeld, "YouTube Declares Victory in Viacom Case," *TechCrunch*, June 23, 2010, http://techcrunch.com/2010/06/23/youtube-declares-victory-in-viacom-case/.

9. For some interesting articles on Better Place and Agassi, see *BusinessWeek*'s profile of Agassi and the *New Yorker* piece on electronic carmaker Tesla, in which the luxury maker is contrasted with Better Place; Steve Hamm, "The Electric Car Acid Test," *BusinessWeek*, January 24, 2008, http://www.businessweek.com/magazine/content/08_05/

b4069042006924.htm; and Tad Friend, "It's Electric!" *New Yorker*, August 24, 2009, http://archives.newyorker.com/?i=2009-08-24#folio=050 (subscribers only).

10. The media center at Nespresso's Web site offers a press release with its growth compared to the market: http://www1.nespresso.com/mediacenter/.

11. Lynn Hirschberg, "Banksable," *New York Times*, June, 2008, http://www.nytimes.com/2008/06/01/magazine/01tyra-t.html?pagewanted=all.

12. Peretti published his account of the exchange in the April 9, 2001, edition of *The Nation*, http://www.thenation.com/doc/20010409/peretti.

13. See, for example, Greenpeace's 2010 anti-Nestlé campaign protesting the use of palm oil from possibly illegal palm plantations, where it hijacked the Kit Kat brand as a stand-in for Nestlé as a whole.

Conclusion

1. The Espresso Book Machine's self-publishing functionality is enabled through a partnership with Lightning Source. Self-publishers connect to the Lightning Source platform via the Espresso and input their data, and the machine prints and binds the results.

2. Clayton M. Christensen, *The Innovator's Dilemma: When New Technologies Cause Great Firms to Fail* (Boston: Harvard Business School Press, 1997); Clayton M. Christensen, *The Innovator's Solution: Creating and Sustaining Successful Growth* (Boston: Harvard Business School Press, 2004).

3. Peter Corbett, "Facebook Demographics and Statistics Report 2010—145% Growth in 1 Year," iStrategyLabs blog, January 4, 2010, http://www.istrategylabs.com/2010/01/facebook-demographics-and-statistics-report-2010-145-growth-in-1-year/; and Justin Smith, "Fastest Growing Demographic on Facebook: Women over 55," *Inside Facebook*, February 2, 2009, http://www.insidefacebook.com/2009/02/02/fastest-growing-demographic-on-facebook-women-over-55.

4. Study is available at http://www.pewinternet.org/Reports/2010/Mobile-Access-2010.aspx.

5. Data on consumer price sensitivity was derived from the IBM 2010 Digital Consumer Survey.

6. Abbie Griffin, *Drivers of NPD Success: The 1997 PDMA Report* (Mount Laurel, NJ: PDMA Association, 1997).

INDEX

AAA, 73–74
Achatz, Gary, 77
acquisitions, 168–169
advertising
    analytics services and, 158–160
    auction pricing in, 82
    Blyk and, 109–110, 113
    device independence of,
      116–117
    digital, 115–116
    entrenched relationships in, 140
    integrated, 116, 117–118
    mobile, 5
    payer innovation and,
      109–110, 115–120, 136, 179
    product placement/
      sponsorship and, 120–124
    relevance of, 118–119
    segmentation in, 111, 116,
      135–136
    social media, 127–128
    targeted, 180
    TV, audience for, 26–27
    value integration with,
      157–158
    value propositions and,
      135

Agassi, Shai, 49, 161
air travel, pricing in, 87, 100
à la carte pricing, 66, 86–92
Alinea, 77
Amazon, 5
    componentization at, 149, 151
    Kindle, 72, 75–76, 80, 172, 182,
      183
    pricing models at, 75–76, 80,
      90
    Prime, 73
    recommendation relevance
      of, 61
    streaming video by, 40, 89
ambiguity, 168
American Idol, 120
anchor prices, 68–69, 138
Apple, 5
    App Store, 79–80, 150
    componentization at, 149, 150,
      168
    e-books, 172, 182
    iPad, 117, 123–124, 182
    iPhone, 31, 34, 79, 81, 150
    iPod, 29, 79, 123, 150
    iTunes, 27, 41–43, 73, 75, 87,
      89, 90, 151, 189

Apple (*continued*)
  media apps, 123–124
  music innovation by, 153
  Nike+, 29
  pricing models at, 73, 75, 79–80, 87
  simplicity at, 189
  television content in, 89
Apple Store, 149, 168
application programming interfaces (APIs), 151
Armani, 164
Asda, 52
assumptions, 15
AT&T, 91, 168
attitudes
  about consumer base, 176
  toward pricing, 67–70
  toward technology, 36–37
auction pricing models, 81–84
automotive industry
  bundling in, 86
  consumer research in, 28
  information services in, 10, 28–29
  rentals in, 94–95
  segmentation in, 48–49
  value integration in, 160–161
Aviva, 120

BabyCenter, 124
bandwidth, unlimited, 4, 90–91
Banks, Tyra, 145, 163
behavioral approach, to segmentation, 23, 24, 27–32
  in casinos, 49–52
  change in, 175–176
  continuous change in, 36

launching innovation and, 174–178
package innovation and, 167
payer innovation and, 140
personal information data and, 112–120, 128–135
pitfalls in, 54–59
pricing and, 70–75
Ben 10: Alien Force Game Creator, 149
Best Buy, 143–144, 145, 156, 165, 168
Better Place, 48–49, 160–161
Bianchini, Gina, 126
Bild tabloid, 71
Blockbuster Video, 21–22, 23, 40, 56
  kiosk rentals by, 94
  recommendations by, 62–63
Blyk, 5, 109–110, 111, 113, 136
  targeted advertising in, 119
BMG, 74
BMW iDrive, 28–29, 48
books
  e-, 72, 75–76, 80, 182, 183
  Espresso Book Machine and, 35–36, 171–172, 185–187
"bottom of the pyramid," 156
brands
  extending, 162–164
  Massive Passives and, 33–34
  negative associations with, 163–164
  personality-driven, 145
British National Health Service, 82–83
Brown, Tim, 15
bundling, 86–92, 99

Index

business models
  criticality of innovation
    in, 11–12
  definition of, 6
  disruption of, 1–3
  enterprise innovation
    approach to, 6, 7
  IBM framework for
    innovation in, 6, 7
  industry innovation approach
    to, 6–7
  innovations in, 6
  revenue innovation approach
    to, 6, 8–9

cable television, 2
  bundling in, 87–92
  content providers in, 88–89
  pricing models in, 79
  two-way information in, 58
Cablevision, 2
Canal+, 89
cannibalization
  componentization and, 147
  film industry, 204
  pricing models and, 67, 76
  revenue model innovation
    and, 55
Cartoon Network Digital,
  148–149
casinos, 49–52
Castrol Complete, 155–156
celebrities, 162–163
change management, 188–191
Charles Schwab, 96–98, 103–104
Christensen, Clayton, 22, 175
CIGNA, 84
Clooney, George, 121
Coca-Cola Company, 78, 121

coffee industry, 161–162
Coffee Pod, 162
collaboration, 104, 168–169
Collins, Jim, 9
Combs, Sean, 162
Comcast, 89, 90–91, 177
communications, ubiquitous
  low-cost, 4, 9–12, 47–49
comparison shopping, 28, 97,
  103–104
componentization, 144–145,
  146–152, 165
  challenges in, 166
  mash-ups, 145, 150–152
  at Nike, 167–168
  pricing by parts and, 85
Condé Nast, 124, 157, 158
conflict management, 139
congestion pricing, 76–77
consumers. *See* customers
content
  device independence of, 89,
    116–117
  independence of, 27–28, 60–61
  pricing models and, 72
continuity pricing, 74–75
Converse, 163–164
cost-sharing models, 84
Courtyard by Marriott, 124
Craigslist, 177
Crossing the Chasm
  (Moore), 30
cross-subsidy models, 76, 78–81,
  182–183
culture, corporate, 188–189
customers, 8
  attitudes of toward price, 67–70
  buying power of, 56–57
  data collection on, 58–59
  existing, 174

customers (*continued*)
    expectations of, 4, 9–12,
       27–32, 98
    information available to, 28
    innovation and, 174–178
    options of, 24
    personal information of,
       119–120
    price training of, 68–69
    product redefinition and,
       160–161
    revenue innovation and, 22–23
    satisfaction and loyalty of,
       85–86, 155–156
    segmentation of, 14, 17, 21–64,
       174–178
    taste in choices by, 29–30
    trust and, 58–59
    young, desirability of, 113
customization
    of grocery coupons, 53–54
    Kool Kids and, 35
    of segmentation, 31
    segmentation and, 54

data processing power, 4, 9–12
    improvements in, 61–63
    personal information and,
       119–120, 128–135
    segmentation and, 58–59
Datek, 97
Day, George, 15
decline, stages of, 9
Deutsche Telekom, 71
device independence, 89, 116–117
Digiboo, 182
digitization
    advertising and, 115–116
    behavioral change and, 44–45

comparison shopping and, 97
componentization and, 144–145
content independence and,
    27–28, 60–61, 72, 115–116
music industry and, 39
pricing by parts and, 84–85
product life cycles and, 167
subscription models and, 70–75
windowing and, 44
direct revenue models, 112–114
discounting models, 84
Disney, Walt, 14
Disney stores, 149, 168
dynamic pricing, 77–78, 100

early adopters, 30
early majority, 30
eBay, 82
e-books, 72, 75–76, 80, 182, 183
Economist, 100
education, 37
E-Loan, 82
EMI, 122–123
energy epicures, 47
energy stalwarts, 46
enterprise innovation, 6, 7
environmental awareness,
    155–156, 163–164
Espresso Book Machine, 35–36,
    171–172, 185–187
E*Trade, 97
expectations
    for consumer control, 4
    of customers, 4, 9–12, 27–32,
      98, 180
    media consumer, 27–31
    of relevance, 180
    for services, 98
Expedia, 126

Facebook, 110, 127–128, 129
   componentization in, 151
   e-commerce in, 129–130
   Places, 130–131
   privacy and, 128, 135
   user demographics, 175
fashion rentals, 65–66, 92, 95
fast followers, 30
Federer, Roger, 121–122
fee-based indirect revenues, 110,
   120–124
   white labeling, 110, 124–126
film industry, 101–102. *See also*
   video rental industry
financial services, 37
   pricing models in, 73, 97–98,
   103–104, 181
   product integration in, 183
   segmentation and
     personalization in, 63
   white labeling in, 125
Financial Times, 5, 44, 71,
   100
First Response pregnancy
   tests, 124
flexibility, 168
flooring industry innovations, 155
Ford Sync, 10, 28–29, 183
Foursquare, 130, 136, 152
fragmentation of markets, 156
Frank, Ronald, 25
freemiums, 44, 76, 80–81
Fresh Direct, 73
From Bags to Riches, 95
frugal goal seekers, 46–47

Gadgetiers, 34, 36–37, 48
   bundling and, 87–88
   willingness of to pay, 176

gambling industry, 37, 49–52
Gannett Company, 124, 132–134
Gawker Media, 5
GE, 154
Geek Squad, 143–144, 145,
   156, 165
GE Money, 125
General Motors (GM), 10, 28–29
Gillette, 79
GM, Tahoe social media
   campaign, 62
Go City Kids, 134
Google, 5, 7
   AdSense, 82
   analytics services at, 158–160
   brand extension at, 164
   componentization at, 151
   ContentID technology,
     158–159, 166
   Earth, 152
   location-based services in, 131
   relevance improvement at, 61
   rights management in, 166
   Talk, 102
   TV, 89
gouging, price, 78
GPS systems, 28–29
Griffin, Abbie, 184
grocery stores, 52–54, 73, 125
Groupon, 131–132

Hanaro Telecom, 88–89
Harrah's, 51–52
Harvard Business Review
   Press, 85
health care, 37
   electronic records in, 10–11
   package innovation in, 184
   pay-for-performance in, 82–84

health care (*continued*)
  pricing models in, 74, 82–84,
    181
Hearst, 157
"Help Vince," 131
Hesse, Thomas, 57
hospitality industry, 78, 147
How the Mighty Fall (Collins), 9
Hulu, 5, 87, 90
  advertising in, 116–117
  payer innovation in,
    136, 139
  platform innovation at, 177
  pricing models of, 180, 181, 190
human dynamics, 4

IBM
  on advertising, 180
  Digital Consumer Survey,
    59–60, 114, 176
  Institute for Business Value,
    11–12, 32, 45–49
  segmentation model of, 31–32
  Smarter Planet concept, 11
IDEO, 15
incumbents, 177–178
  pricing innovation and,
    98–99
  revenue innovation for,
    22–23
indirect revenue, 111–112, 139.
    See also payer innovation
industry innovation, 6–7
industry transformations, 8–9
inertia, 97
information, ubiquity of, 11
  automotive industry and, 161
  car consumers and, 28

customer segmentation
    and, 17
  revenue management and, 139
  two-way flow of, 58–59
information sharing, 137
infrastructure
  package innovation and, 169
  payer innovation and, 125, 141
  pricing and, 97, 106–107
  segmentation and, 64
innovation. *See also* package
    innovation; payer innovation;
    pricing innovation; revenue
    model innovations
  in business models, 6
  CEO focus on, 11–12
  copying, 55–56
  criticality of, 11–12
  experiments in, 184–187
  launching, 171–192
  organizational structure and,
    188–191
  product, 38
  segmentation and, 174–178
  speed of, 4
  success criteria in, 190
  talent for, 189
innovators, 30
The Innovator's Dilemma
    (Christensen), 175
The Innovator's Solution
    (Christensen), 175
integration
  of advertising, 116, 117–118,
    135–136
  of e-commerce, 129
  value, 145
intellectual property rights, 166
Interface flooring, 155

Internet
    anchor prices and, 68–69, 138
    componentization and,
        144–145
    data traffic on, 91–92
    freemiums on, 81
    free services on, 1–3
    as news source, 175
    of things, 11, 29
    Web applications, 152
Intuit, 80–81
inventory management, 97
iPad, 117, 123–124, 182
iPod/iPhone, 175
    componentization and, 150
    MapMyFitness app for, 81
    Nike+ for, 29
    print media apps for,
        123–124
    subscription models and, 71
iTunes, 41, 42, 87, 189
    pricing model of, 73, 75, 90
    television shows in, 89

Jay-Z, 123
Jobs, Steve, 149
Johnson & Johnson, 25, 82–83,
    124

K-Cups, 162
Kindle, 72, 75–76, 80, 182
kiosk model, 56, 92–94
Komisar, Randy, 79
Kool Kids, 34–35, 36–37
    personal information sharing
        by, 119–120
    willingness of to pay, 176

laggards, 30
late majority, 30
Leanback, 175–176
LendingTree, 82
Leno, Jay, 38–39
Lenovo, 121
Lexus, 158
LG, 157
Li & Fung, 7
Lightning Source, 187
Live Nation, 123
Living Social, 131–132
Loblaws supermarkets, 125
location-based data, 118,
    130–131, 152
Lopez, Jennifer, 162
loyalty cards, 52–54
Lucky magazine, 129

magazines
    cost to produce, 69
    e-commerce and, 129
    pricing models for, 72
    product sponsorship in,
        123–124
    value integration in, 157–158
MagHound, 72
mainstream users, 30
MapMyFitness, 81
MapMyRun, 81
Marks & Spencer, 52
mash-ups, 145, 150–152, 165, 166
Maslow, Abraham, 25
Massey, William, 25
Massive Passives, 33–34,
    36–37, 48
    behavior change in, 175–176
    bundling and, 87–88

Massive Passives (*continued*)
  technology savvy of, 59–60
  willingness of to pay, 176
media industry, 3–15
  audience fragmentation in,
    26–27
  componentization in, 147–149
  content options in, 27
  external trends driving, 4
  incumbents versus new
    entrants in, 177–178
  lessons from, 13–15, 45–54,
    191–192
  payer innovation in, 179
  pricing models in, 181
  revenue disruption in, 2
  revenue innovation in, 9
  revenue opportunities in, 44–45
  segmentation in, 26–27,
    31–35, 32–35, 40–43
  sponsorship in, 123–124
  successes in, 5
  success/failure distribution in,
    12–14
Merck, 83, 84
metered models, 44, 71
microfinance institutions,
  156–157
Microsoft, 7, 117, 150–151, 183
Mint, 80–81
Mitchell, Arnold, 25
MomsLikeMe.com, 132–134, 136
monetization, 127, 177–178
Moore, Geoffrey, 30
Morning Joe, 120
Murdoch, Rupert, 104
Murrow, Edward, 120
music industry
  componentization in, 85,
    147–148

digitization in, 39
direct revenue model in, 112
flexibility in, 168
mash-ups in, 150–151
pricing models in, 85–86, 99,
  102, 113–114, 181
product sponsorship in,
  122–123
revenue opportunities in, 44–45
rights management in, 166
streaming, 113–114
value integration in, 153–154
white labeling in, 125

Napster, 42, 43, 73
NBC, 38–39
Nespresso, 161–162
Netflix, 21–22, 39–40, 56
  new releases in, 93
  pricing model of, 73, 90
  recommendation engine
    of, 137
  streaming video by, 89
News Corporation, 60
newspapers. *See also Financial
  Times*; *New York Times*;
  Times (London)
  cost to produce, 69
  payer models in, 138
  premiums for early
    editions, 60
  pricing models for, 71,
    100
New York Public Library, 186
New York Times, 2, 70
  platform innovation at, 177
  pricing models of, 75, 104,
    180, 181
  subscription model of, 71

Nickelodeon, 134
Nike, 29, 121–122, 163, 164,
    167–168
Ning, 126–127
Norwich Union, 120
Novartis, 83
Now TV, 89

O'Brien, Conan, 38–39
Olympics, 121
On Demand Books (ODB),
    171–172, 187
OnStar, 10, 28–29
operations
    package innovation and, 170
    payer innovation and, 141
    pricing and, 107
    segmentation and, 64
opportunities, finding, 176–177
organizational dynamics, 4
organizational structure, 188–191

package innovation, 14, 17,
    143–170, 179, 182–184
    componentization models, 85,
        146–152, 165, 166
    customer limitations and, 26
    definition of, 144
    getting started in, 169–170
    lessons in, 166–169
    mash-ups, 145, 165, 166
    pitfalls in, 164–166
    rights management and, 166
    skills for, 165–166
    timing in, 165
    value extensions, 145, 162–164
    value integration, 144–146,
        153–162

Pandora, 5
Parents Connect, 134
partnerships, 168–169
parts pricing, 66, 84–86
passive rate payers, 47
Pay As You Drive programs,
    120
payer innovation, 14, 16–17,
    109–141
    ad-supported, 110, 115–120
    definition of, 110
    direct revenue models and,
        112–114
    fee-based, 110, 120–124
    by industry, 179–180
    lessons in, 138–140
    pitfalls in, 134–137
    product placement and
        sponsorship in, 110,
        120–124
    in social media, 110
    social networking and,
        127–135
    third parties in, 110–112
    white labeling, 110, 124–126
pay-for-performance models,
    81–84
pay-per-use models, 73–74
pay-per-view models, 88–89
paywall model, 2
pay-what-you-want pricing,
    81–84
peer-to-peer sharing, 3, 40–43
People magazine, 129
Peretti, Jonah, 167
Peripheral Vision (Day), 15
personal information, 112–120,
    128–135
    targeted advertising and,
        136–137

personalization
consumer expectation for,
4, 11
segmentation and, 57–58,
60–61
Personics, 41
pharmaceutical firms, pricing
models in, 82–84
piracy, 3, 40–43
placements, product, 110,
120–124
platform models, 151, 177. *See
also* componentization
Please Rob Me, 152
Prahalad, C. K., 156
President's Choice brand, 125
Priceline, 82
pricing innovation, 14, 16,
65–107, 180–182
anchor prices and, 68–69,
138
bundling versus à la carte,
86–92
continuity, 74–75
cross-subsidies, 76, 78–81
dynamic pricing, 77–78, 100
ease of operation and, 176
factors driving, 101–102
getting started in, 104, 106
in grocery chains, 53–54
incumbents versus new
entrants and, 98–99
iTunes, 42
lessons in, 102–104
by parts, 84–86
pitfalls in, 96–102
psychology in, 99–100
razor blade models, 79–80
rent versus buy models, 92–97
segmentation and, 70, 102–104

service level and, 98
subscription models, 70–75,
100–101
tiered pricing, 76, 80–81
user-controlled models, 81–84
variable pricing, 75–84, 100
what and when to pay, 66–70
Primedic, 74
privacy policies, 128, 135
Procter & Gamble, 25, 120
products
different pricing models for,
66–67
digital versus physical, 9–10
life cycles of, 167
placement/sponsorship of,
110, 120–124
price to produce, 69
redefining, value integration
and, 160–162
value extensions and, 162–164
professional gamblers, 51
Progressive Insurance, 119–120

Quicken, 80–81

Radiohead, 82
razor blade model of pricing,
79, 162
reverse, 79–80
recognition seekers, 51
Redbox, 5, 56, 92–94, 204
relevance
of advertising, 118–119, 180
consumer expectation for,
4, 11, 180
data collection technologies
and, 61–63

product sponsorship and,
    122–123
rental pricing models, 65–66,
    92–96, 155. *See also* video
    rental industry
Rent the Runway, 65–66, 92, 95
revenue model innovations, 6,
    8–9, 172–174. *See also* payer
    innovation
  cannibalization by, 55
  diversification and, 139
  free Internet services and,
    1–3
  for incumbents versus new
    entrants, 22–23
  indirect, 111–112
  interim needs and, 35–36
  in media, 44–45
  media industry lessons on, 2,
    3–15
  metered models, 44
  music industry, 40–43
  packaging in, 14, 17, 146
  payer, 14, 16–17
  porting existing models, 177
  pricing, 14, 16, 99
  segmentation, 14, 22–24,
    35–40, 55–59
  trends affecting, 9–12
  types of, 15–19
reward seekers, 51
rights management, 166
ringtones, 148
risk
  in package innovation,
    165–166
  package innovation and,
    167–168
  pricing and, 97–98
Rocawear, 123

Sainsbury's, 52
Sam's Club, 53–54
SAP, 147
SCVNGR, 131
seasonal businesses, 96
segmentation, 14, 17, 21–64,
    174–178
  advertising and, 111
  by age and sex, 26–27
  automotive industry, 48–49
  basis in, 25
  behavioral approach to, 23, 24,
    27–32
  in casinos, 49–52
  by consumption volume,
    31–32
  continuous change in, 36
  by degree of interaction, 31, 32
  demographic, geographic,
    socioeconomic, 25–26, 133
  difficulty of, 57–58
  by format choice, 31
  getting started in, 63–64
  in grocery chains, 52–54
  history of, 24–27
  for incumbents versus new
    entrants, 22–23
  lessons on, 59–63
  in media, 26–27, 31–35, 40–43
  of media consumers, 32–35
  pitfalls in, 54–59
  pricing and, 70, 102–104
  product use differences and,
    30–32
  psychographic, 25
  purpose of, 25
  in revenue innovation, 22–24
  revenue models for, 35–40
  for technology consumption,
    30

segmentation (*continued*)
  utility industry, 45–49
  VALS, 25, 26
sell-through industries, 95–96
service
  contracts for, 155–156
  expectations for, 98
service-ization, 154–156
services, packaging, 143–144,
    154–156
Sezmi, 89, 182
ShopSavvy, 96
silos, information sharing and,
    137–138, 178–179
Skype, 81, 102
Slim, Carlos, 70
Smarter Planet concept, 11
smart homes, 47
smart meters, 46, 184
Smith, Wendell, 24
socializers, 51
social media, 62
  componentization in, 151
  location-based, 130–131
  payer innovation in, 110,
    127–135
  user demographics, 175–176
  white labeling in, 126–127
social responsibility, 155–156,
    163–164
software
  B2B, 183
  componentization of,
    146–147, 150–151
  pricing models for, 80–81
  service packaging with, 154
software as a service (SaaS)
    models, 154
Sony, 57, 183
sponsorships, 110, 120–124, 179

sports industry, product
    sponsorship in, 121–122
Spotify, 5, 113–114, 139, 181
Springer, Axel, 71
start-ups
  media industry, 177–178
  pricing innovation by, 98–99
  revenue innovation for,
    22–23
*Star Wars: The Clone Wars Game
    Creator*, 148–149
Stefani, Gwen, 162
Stewart, Martha, 145, 162–163
strategy
  package innovation and, 169
  payer innovation and, 140–141
  pricing and, 106
  segmentation and, 63–64
Style Finder, 129
subscription models, 66, 70–75
  bundling in, 87–92
  car rental, 94–95
  channel balance in, 100–101
  unlimited consumption,
    100–101
success, criteria for, 190
Sugar Mama, 135

taxi industry, targeted ads in,
    118, 136
technology
  attitudes toward, 36–37
  consumer segments for, 30,
    36–37
  improvements in data
    collection, 61–63
  rapid change in, 4, 9–12
  segmentation based on,
    32–35

service packaging with,
143–144
user demographics, 175–176
telecommunications market,
102, 183
payer innovation in, 109–110
revenue models in, 112–113
ringtones in, 148
VOIP and, 81, 102
Tesco, 52–54
tiered pricing, 76, 80–81,
113–114. *See also* freemiums
Time Inc., 2, 124
timeliness, consumer
expectation for, 4, 11
Time magazine, 2
Times (London), 180, 181
Time Warner Cable, 90–91,
168
timing, 165, 167
TiVo, 79
Tonight Show, 38–39
Toyota, 161
transparency, 104
travel industry, 37
pricing models in, 78
white labeling in, 126
trust, customer data and,
58–59
TurboTax, 80
TV Everywhere, 89, 177
Twitter, 129, 151, 152

uncertainty, 167–168
UNICEF, 121
Unilever, 156–157
unit-cost revenue model, 37
Up in the Air, 121
USA Today, 124

user-controlled pricing models,
81–84
utilities, consumer
pricing models in, 181–182,
184
segmentation for, 36–37,
45–49

value chain
collaboration in, 104
fluidity of, 153
package innovation along,
182–184
revenue opportunities in,
44–45
value creation
business models and, 6
package innovation and, 17
packaging and, 144–146
payer innovation and, 135–136
willingness to pay for, 69–70
value delivery, 6
value extensions, 145,
162–164, 165
value integration, 145,
153–162, 165
analytics services and,
158–160
in media, 157–158
through product redefinition,
160–162
Values and Lifestyle (VALS)
methodology, 25, 26, 57
variable pricing models, 66,
75–84, 100
simple, 76–77
Velcade, 82–83
Vessel Tracker, 152
video games, 5, 90, 148–149

video rental industry, 5, 21–22,
23, 39–40, 56
  rent versus buy in, 92–94
  streaming and, 91–92
Virgin, 6–7
VOIP, 81, 102

Wall Street Journal, 60, 80,
100–101
Walmart, 52–54, 93, 117–118,
129, 180
Warner Music, 2
Web 2.0 technologies, 61–62
Wharton School of Business,
42–43
white labeling, 110, 124–126
Wii, 90

Williams, Robbie, 122–123
Wilson, Fred, 80
Wind, Yoram, 25
windowing, 44, 62, 72
Winfrey, Oprah, 145
World Bank, 187

Xbox, 90, 117
Xerox, 187

YouTube, 87, 147, 158–160
  Leanback, 175–176

Zara, 7
Zillion TV, 44, 182
Zipcar, 49, 94–95

ACKNOWLEDGMENTS

I've been a consultant for some thirty years now, so "writing" in PowerPoint is pretty much second nature, as is the brainstorming necessary to create new ideas and the public speaking required to deliver them. Prose, however, is a very different thing, so the idea of writing a book was a bit intimidating. I therefore owe a great deal of gratitude to the many who encouraged and supported the effort.

I must first thank Kirsten Sandberg, my first editor at Harvard Business Press, who literally discovered me when I was speaking and moderating an HBS panel. Kirsten helped me turn my conceptual ideas into a proposal and guided me through the process of supplementing my knowledge and skills so I could complete the project. Her efforts were enhanced at the Press by Jacqueline Murphy, who worked with me in the final stages of writing to shape, edit, and improve the manuscript. Finally, let me thank Justin Fox and his broader team, who as the editorial director at Harvard Business Press helped me see the project to its conclusion and publication.

The manuscript could not have been completed without my superb editorial support team of Tim Ogden and Laura Starita from Sona Partners. They were my collaborators, both challenging me and contributing as we proceeded. They kept me on schedule and taught me how my thought processes, precepts, and prior publications could be combined into a final, coherent whole. Without them, this would still be a work in progress.

The foundation of this book consists of the research and publications I have created over the past several years with my Strategy/Media & Entertainment colleagues at IBM. Prime among my collaborators at IBM is Bill Battino, my fellow partner for the past fourteen years and coauthor of most of my recent Media & Entertainment (M&E) publications. Louisa Shipnuck and Karen Feldman acted as research leaders and coauthors for most of these efforts. I also share credit with Karen for much of the conceptual thinking that led to this book. Karen was at my side as a dedicated collaborator in developing and shaping the research for the book itself. I also thank Eric Mark, who was a dedicated staff member and contributor to some of our early media research, and staff members Mike Ash, Nadia Leonelli, and Seth Miller for their support of our research.

I want to acknowledge as well the support of our IBM M&E Industry general manager Steve Canepa and his predecessor Dick Anderson, as well as Steve Abraham, our consulting Global M&E Industry leader and fellow industry partner. All three sponsored the research and took part in the brainstorming that shaped the ideas and challenged my thinking. Other partners, past and present, made significant contributions and participated in client interviews, including Susan Goldsmith, Cheryl Grise, Martin Guillaume, Edward Hanapole, David Jensen, William Maloney,

Acknowledgments

William Serrao, Adam Steinberg, Niko Waesche, and Richard Whittington.

The terrific IBM business research group, the IBM Institute for Business Value (IBV), sponsors all of our business research efforts. I greatly value the support and encouragement of its leader and my close friend, Peter Korsten, who offered ideas and support whenever it was needed. I would also like to acknowledge the Communications IBV sector leader at the time, Ekow Nelson, for help in framing some of the research and supporting my efforts with his team.

This book builds broadly on our strategy practice research, since it takes examples and points to other industries that can learn from our experience in M&E. I would like to thank my partners past and present on our CEO study and global leadership team over the past several years: Marc Chapman, Grace Chopard, Steven Davidson, Hans-Henrik Jorgensen, Sara Longworth, David Lubowe, Ranier Mehl, Matt Porta, Eric Riddleberger, and Michel Vlasselaer for their contributions to these efforts. The CEO research continues to uncover relevant insight due to the diligent support of CEO study program director Ragna Bell, who has supported me in this and much of our strategy research. She has been my coauthor, along with Edward Giesen and Eric Riddleberger, on our IBM papers on business models. We in turn were supported by our other business strategy leaders, such as Ron Frank and Greg Morris. Also, I thank Denise Arnette, who has worked with our strategy team leadership and me over many years in these and other development efforts. Keith Landis and Christian Slike have driven our marketing efforts and taught us about the importance of eminence, which drove many of our prior publications and any such success we have achieved.

My involvement in strategy consulting over the past twenty-five-plus years has given me the opportunity to work with some of the best minds on some of the most pressing business issues of the past three decades. From my early days debating issues as an intern with Bruce Henderson, BCG's legendary leader, to addressing the challenges of my automotive clients of the 1980s, to advising my retail and media clients from the 1990s through today, the learning process has been constant and the challenges ever changing. Such is the stimulation on which I thrive and what makes this all worthwhile.

The CEOs, COOs, and strategic planners who have been my clients and participated in our studies have greatly contributed to my development and success. Seeing their struggles and challenges firsthand has provided a test bed for the content that has evolved into this book. They are too many to name individually, and I have promised not to quote anyone without express permission. Nonetheless, I would like to acknowledge them all. I hope I have a made a contribution to their thinking and business success.

Of course I cannot leave out Adam Klaber, my leader in my current role at IBM. He and Jim Bramante gave me the opportunity to be the Global and Americas strategy leader at IBM, and they encouraged me to keep growing to a new and higher level. Adam encouraged my efforts and created the working environment for me to accomplish the objectives of this project. Adam's leadership, together with the vision and challenge of our Global Business Services general managers, Ginni Rometty and now Frank Kern, have sustained my inquisitiveness and energy throughout the project.

Projects like this do not get completed without the efforts of team members who can keep me at a frenetic pace. I thank my executive assistants during my times at IBM—Michelle Craigen, Anita Duffaut, Kevi Jones, and Hidemi Takada-Fulcher—for making it all work and happen somewhat near as planned.

Finally, the strong support of family and friends is key to any sustained effort. For me it started with my parents, Leona and Sherwood, who stimulated my thinking, taught me to be inquisitive, and encouraged me to believe I could be whatever I wanted to be. My loving wife Jann sacrificed a significant share of my time, yet still gave me her constant belief and support. Our partnership, her shameless promotion of me, and her constant emotional and enthusiastic support make all this possible and rewarding. Finally there is my daughter Ashley, who has been my test market of one from childhood into young adulthood. It sometimes embarrassed her to have me share our family experiences in presentations, but I owe a great deal of my ability to stay current with the Kool Kids by watching her behaviors and choices, as well as those of her younger cousins. To them and to my broader circle of family and friends, I say thanks for your love and for being there with me through the ups and downs.

ABOUT THE AUTHOR

Saul J. Berman is the Vice President and Global Strategy Consulting Leader of IBM Global Business Services. He has more than twenty-five years of consulting experience, working closely with major corporations around the globe on strategic business issues.

Berman has dealt extensively with issues of competitive positioning, differentiation, new business plans and strategies, new business models, growth, operational and cost improvement, operations/manufacturing strategy, organizational design, and enterprise transformation. His clients have included most of the major media companies as well as Internet companies, telecommunication companies, consumer goods manufacturers, retailers, and automotive companies in the United States, Japan, Europe, and Australia. A frequent speaker to industry and strategic planning organizations such as the World Economic Forum, MIPCOM, Consumer Electronics Association, McGraw-Hill Media Summit, the National Association of Broadcasters, Online Publishers Association, and Digital Hollywood, Berman was named one of the Top 25 Consultants of 2005 by *Consulting* magazine.

Previously, Berman served as an assistant professor of management at the University of Southern California, started his consulting career at Boston Consulting Group, and led the Strategy practice at PwC Consulting. He has served as a board member of the USC Film School Entertainment Technology Center and of the Southern California chapter of the Strategic Leadership Forum.

Berman has authored or coauthored numerous books and white papers, including *Rethinking the Enterprise* (2010), *Beyond Advertising* (2009), *Succeeding in the New Economic Environment* (2009), *Rethinking Innovation* (2008), *The End of Advertising as We Know It* (2007), *Paths to Success: Three Ways to Innovate Your Business Model* (2007), and *The End of Television as We Know It* (2005). He has also been featured in publications such as the *Wall Street Journal,* the *New York Times, Bloomberg Businessweek,* and *Forbes.*

Berman holds a PhD in management and information systems and an MBA in production systems and operations research from the Columbia Business School. He obtained a bachelor of science in economics at The Wharton School of the University of Pennsylvania.